HERITAGE
OF THE SEA

MARITIME HISTORY TITLES BY THE SAME AUTHOR

HERITAGE OF THE SEA

Famous Preserved Ships around the UK

Peter C. Smith

Pen & Sword
MARITIME

First published in 1974 by Balfour Books, Cambridge.

This edition published in Great Britain in 2012 by
Pen & Sword Maritime
an imprint of
Pen & Sword Books Ltd
47 Church Street
Barnsley
South Yorkshire
S70 2AS

ISBN: 978-1-84884-646-3

Typeset in 11/13pt Palatino by
Concept, Huddersfield, West Yorkshire

Printed and bound in India by
Replika Press Pvt. Ltd.

Pen & Sword Books Ltd incorporates the Imprints of Pen & Sword Aviation, Pen & Sword
Family History, Pen & Sword Maritime, Pen & Sword Military, Pen & Sword Discovery,
Wharncliffe Local History, Wharncliffe True Crime, Wharncliffe Transport, Pen & Sword Select,
Pen & Sword Military Classics, Leo Cooper, The Praetorian Press, Remember When,
Seaforth Publishing and Frontline Publishing.

For a complete list of Pen & Sword titles please contact
PEN & SWORD BOOKS LIMITED
47 Church Street, Barnsley, South Yorkshire, S70 2AS, England
E-mail: enquiries@pen-and-sword.co.uk
Website: www.pen-and-sword.co.uk

CONTENTS

INTRODUCTION

The history of Great Britain is in itself a history of the sea and sea power. The sea brought to our shores many invaders, the Romans, the Danes, the Viking raiders, and from the earliest days of recorded history it served us by bringing trade from the Mediterranean. It has always been this nation's main artery, secure if guarded and exposed if, as today, neglected.

That this tiny island race could have developed into the greatest world empire ever known was due exclusively to the dominance of the sea which was exercised between the seventeenth and early twentieth centuries. That dominance was abandoned by uncomprehending politicians in the 1920s and today, almost a century on, remains but a dim and fading memory but, while it lasted, it ensured that no invader between the coming of the Normans and the end of the Second World War, violated our freedoms, although the books are full of tyrants who have tried from the Spanish Armada, through the Dutch Wars, the towering ambitions of Napoleon, the Kaiser and Hitler, all of whom overran and enslaved their continental opponents only to stand gazing frustrated across the narrow gap of the Straits of Dover. Both the *Grande Armée* of France and the Panzers of Germany were stopped in their tracks by the sea and the British seamen who controlled it. Since 1945, however, our borders have lain open to anyone and everyone.

Conversely, by exercising that earlier easy domination over the world's sea routes, Great Britain was able to utilise her trading skills and technical innovation to the full and for centuries London was the trading centre of the world. Britain led the world in every aspect of maritime invention during the eighteenth, nineteenth and first decade of the twentieth centuries, from the ships of the line, through the ironclads to the *Dreadnought* in warship design and from the *Great Britain* to the famous Cunard liners in the mercantile world.

Sadly all this has been thrown away in the last sixty years but the seafaring instinct and tradition still lingers in many parts of the population and it has been gradually realised over the last half-century what a priceless heritage still exists in what is left of our famous old ships. Although the realisation came too late for many, superb examples of the maritime skill for which this nation was so renowned have been saved from the breakers' yards for the enjoyment and education of future generations. Sadly, since the first edition of this book, many included therein have, to the nation's shame, been allowed to go, the *Arethusa*, the *Chrysanthemum* among them, and scandalously the National Maritime Museum has 'dispersed' to use their accountant-speak words, the last steam-driven tug, *Reliant* (the former *Old Trafford*), instead of caring for her; meanwhile others just as valuable to the nation, are under grave threat. Some, such as the famous 1934 J-Class yacht, Britain's 1934 America's Cup contender *Endeavour I*, still exist, but not, unfortunately, in the UK. It is hoped that this book, which records just a selection of some of the most famous of these ancient vessels and illustrates them in full colour photography, will spur others to do what they can to assist in this worthwhile task. The Heritage of the Sea is our heritage, and it is a proud and honoured one.

Many people gave generously of their time and expertise in helping me with this book, I would like to thank them all for their kindness, cemented by a mutual desire to record for posterity the best of what little is left of our nautical history against total Government and much public indifference. So my gratitude to the following for both original research back in 1974 and current research in 2012 –

Richard Basey, The *MTB102* Trust, Lowestoft; Vice Admiral Sir Patrick Bayly KBE CB DSC, The Maritime Trust; Commander Blake, The Great Britain Project, Bristol; Basil Brambleby, The *Cambria* Trust, Faversham; Dr Phil and Molly Brown, for photographs of *Trincomalee*; Mark and Cathy Chapman, The Cambria Trust; Stephen Courtney, The National Museum of the Royal Navy, Portsmouth; David Cowan, The Tall Ship at Riverside, Glasgow; Ashley Dace, for photographs of *Lydia Eva* and *Mincarlo*; Jacqueline Davis, Portsmouth, for truly outstanding help and detailed information of the *Warrior*; Colin Dixon, Charrington & Company Limited, London; Bernard D. Emson, Secretary British Ship Adoption Society, London; Major J. A. Forsythe TD, Norfolk Wherry Trust; Commander Goddard, Royal Navy, for inviting me aboard the *Cavalier* for her final run to Chatham back in July 1972; Paul H. Gowman, The Norfolk Wherry Trust; Captain R. C. C. Greenless RN, The Maritime Trust; Richard Halton, The *Medway Queen* Preservation Society, Gillingham, Kent; Alison Harris, Honourable Company of Master Mariners, London; A. A. C. Hedges, Curator East Anglian Maritime Museum, Norwich; Brian Horton, The *Foudroyant* Trust; Mark Hyland for his photographs of *Bronington* and *Plymouth*; Sarah Kinloch, *Waverley* and *Balmoral* Excursions Ltd, Bristol; Peter McCann for his photographs of *Waverley*; Alexander 'Sandy' McClearn for his photographs of *Onyx*; Allan McKever for photographs of *Discovery*; John Megoran, Paddle Steamer *Kingswear Castle*, Chatham; J. B. Millar, The Paddle Steam Preservation Society; Richard Pope, Great Western Dockyard, Bristol; Dawn and Sean Rayment, Hinton Ampner, Hants., for some photographs of *Victory* and *Warrior*; Casey Rust, Royal Yacht *Britannia* Trust, Leith; Eileen Skinner; The *Gipsy Moth* Trust, Uppingham; Roderick Stewart, The *Unicorn* Preservation Society, Dundee; Mark Thomas for his photo of HMS *Plymouth*; Lieutenant Commander W. M. Thornton RNR Case Secretary of Shaftesbury Homes; David L. Wright; and special thanks to the duty staff at Chatham Historic Dockyard during my visit in October 2011, from gatehouse keeper to guides they could not have been more courteous and helpful. Finally, my special thanks and gratitude to my Editor, Richard Doherty, for his expertise and wise words.

Peter C. Smith
Riseley
Bedford
2012

BELFAST

Although, *not*, as is so often described, the largest cruiser ever built for the Royal Navy, the *Belfast*, on her completion in 1939, was the largest ship of that classification in the service to be armed with 15.2cm (6-inch) guns. She was also the last big ship to be built of steel with the stronger peace-time specifications and she is a natural, if not the most ideal, representative warship of her type to be preserved. In simple fact, many other vessels of equal or greater distinction had been sold, scrapped or deteriorated to such an extent that she was the only one capable of being preserved.

The *Belfast* had a very distinguished fighting life during her active service with the fleet and was, in lieu of a battleship, a suitable vessel for such preservation. Several American battleships have been saved, as well as a Japanese vessel, Admiral Togo's flagship, the *Mikuma*; but the Imperial War Museum was only able to retain two 38.1cm (15-inch) naval guns, one from each of two of Britain's scrapped battleship fleet, and

The Second World War light cruiser HMS *Belfast* permanently moored on the south bank of the Thames above Tower Bridge. (World Copyright Peter C. Smith)

these are displayed on the front lawn of that establishment in Lambeth. *Belfast*, although a much smaller vessel than those great ships, is the last of the 'all-gun' warships which served the country so well in the Second World War.

She is in direct line of descent from the *Caroline*, also described in these pages, and was built as a light cruiser of the pre-war Town class, belonging to the later sub-division of this type, the Edinburgh class. After the strict limitations imposed on Britain by the Washington Naval Treaty in 1921 and the subsequent London Naval Treaties of the 1930s, the Royal Navy found itself with fifteen of the big 20.3cm (8-inch) gunned heavy cruisers of the County class, which were more suitable for employment on the distant trade routes of the Empire across the world. In addition, the aerial threat was to be met by a special type of anti-aircraft cruiser, the Dido class. This left a limited tonnage available for the general duties associated with cruisers which had been put to good use by building the smaller vessels of the Leander and Arethusa classes with six or eight 15.2cm (6-inch) guns, whereby numbers could be had rather than a few larger ships. However, with the introduction in the late 1930s of the Japanese *Mogami* and the American *Brooklyn* types, which each mounted fifteen 15.2cm (6-inch) guns, it was clear that the Admiralty would have to reply or be completely outclassed. The result was the Town

The B mounting triple 15.2cm (6-inch) gun turret of the Second World War light cruiser HMS *Belfast*. (World Copyright Peter C. Smith)

2

class but which still only carried twelve 15.2cm (6-inch) guns.

The reason why the number of guns in the main armament of the *Belfast* and her sister ship, *Edinburgh*, was less than that of foreign cruisers of the same vintage was due to the Admiralty thinking that our new ships should be sufficiently armoured to enable them to withstand a pounding by the 20.3cm (8-inch) guns of heavy cruisers, which meant that the increase in armour had to be compensated for by substituting triple turrets for quadruples.

Originally to be given traditional cruiser names with long and honourable histories behind them, these ships were instead named after cities and towns with the intention of creating public goodwill in the nation and a sop to provincial politicians at a time of financial stringency. Fortunately, the *Belfast* was to add lustre to her name.

Belfast commissioned on 5 August 1939, a few weeks prior to the outbreak of the Second World War, and, on her given displacement she carried four triple 15.2cm (6-inch) gun turrets, two forward two aft, twelve 10.2cm (4-inch) HA[1] anti-aircraft guns, sixteen 2-pounder pom-poms and six 53.34cm (21-inch) torpedo tubes. She had a crew of 761 officers and men, a speed of 32 knots and had been built by Harland & Wolff at Belfast itself. *Belfast* had been launched by Mrs Neville Chamberlain, wife of the then Prime Minister, eighteen months earlier.

She joined the 18th Cruiser Squadron on the outbreak of war and was based at Scapa Flow in the Orkney Islands as part of the British Home Fleet. In October 1939 she intercepted the German blockade runner *Cap Norte* north-west of the Faroes. In November, however, the *Belfast* was heavily damaged by the detonation of a German magnetic mine laid in the Firth of Forth and had to be towed into Rosyth with a broken

back. Her repairs extended over three years, as long as it had taken to build her originally, during which time opportunity was taken to absorb war lessons and she was extensively modified, including large bulges, which provided extra protection against torpedoes and mines, and she did not finally emerge as a fighting ship once more until November 1942, as almost a new vessel.

She joined the Home Fleet once more, which had as one of the main tasks at this time the covering of convoys taking vast quantities of war material to the Soviet Union through the unwelcoming Arctic Ocean. These convoy routes were beset by German U-boats and bombers operating from their bases in occupied Norway and, in addition, were always under the shadow of being suddenly attacked by the major surface warships of the German fleet which included the battleship *Tirpitz*, battle-cruiser *Scharnhorst*, pocket-battleships *Admiral Scheer* and *Lutzow* and heavy cruiser *Admiral Hipper*, whose Norwegian bases were within easy striking range of the massed merchant ships.

During December 1943, while at sea with the cruisers *Norfolk* and *Sheffield*, giving cover to convoys RA55A and JW55B, the *Belfast*, flying the flag of Admiral 'Bob' Burnett, intercepted the *Scharnhorst* as she was searching for the Allied merchant ships. The three cruisers fought several sharp engagements with the German battle-cruiser, keeping her away from the convoys. The battleship *Duke of York* arrived on the scene accompanied by the light cruiser *Jamaica*, and they cut off the German vessel from her base at Altenfjord, to where she tried to flee. Reduced to a shambles by the combined fire of *Duke of York* and the four cruisers, and hit by several torpedoes from eight British destroyers which joined the battle, the *Scharnhorst* sank with heavy loss of life on 26 December. This, the Battle of the North Cape, was the last instance of British heavy ships engaging their opposite numbers in the traditional style and without any contribution by aircraft.

During the early months of 1944, the *Belfast* continued to operate in northern waters escorting the Home Fleet whose aircraft carriers were

---

1. HA = High Angle, which in Royal Navy parlance denoted a naval gun mounting that was capable of elevation in excess of 50 degrees from the horizontal for use against enemy aircraft. It equated with the term AA (anti-aircraft).

conducting a series of air strikes by the Fleet Air Arm against German convoys in Norwegian coastal waters. In June that same year she was selected as flagship of the Normandy landings during the invasion of France and was utilised as a bombardment ship to assist the British, Canadian and American troops ashore. On the successful completion of this service the *Belfast* underwent another prolonged refit, involving some changes in her armament, to equip her for service in the Pacific where the final assaults on Japan were being planned. However, this refit was not completed until July 1945 and by the time she joined the British Pacific Fleet off Tokyo the war against Japan had ended.

Between 1945 and 1947 the *Belfast* remained in Far Eastern waters, not returning to Portsmouth until August 1947. In October she visited Belfast before returning to the Far East once more in December 1948. Here she remained on normal peacetime duties until the North Korean communists suddenly invaded South Korea which led to the outbreak of the Korean War in June 1950. The *Belfast* was among the many ships assigned to the United Nations' forces operating in defence of the democratic Republic of Korea during this period and she carried out numerous bombardments off both coasts of Korea and was only hit once in return, fortunately without serious damage. With the armistice in September 1952,

The superstructure of the Second World War light cruiser HMS *Belfast* showing two twin 40-mm Bofors AA mountings, director and searchlight. (World Copyright Peter C. Smith)

The Second World War light cruiser HMS *Belfast* showing her after superstructure with rear funnel, directors, light AA weapons and X turret. (World Copyright Peter C. Smith)

the *Belfast* returned to Chatham and was paid off into reserve.

The *Belfast* underwent a lengthy and protracted modernisation between 1956 and 1959 including the fitting of an enclosed bridge. She was re-commissioned at Plymouth in May 1959 despite being almost twenty years old. In this condition she served out her final period of Foreign Service, yet again in the Far East. In the summer of 1962 she returned home by way of Guam, Pearl Harbor, San Francisco, Vancouver, the Panama Canal and Trinidad, arriving back in the UK on 19 June 1962. When she re-commissioned in August that same year it was for her final period of active duty on the Home station. She exercised

her reserve crew in the Mediterranean before paying off for the last time at Devonport on 24 August 1963.

Then she lay in various harbours in a reserve fleet capacity between then and 1971 when she was moved to Fareham Creek, the last resting place of warships awaiting the breakers' yard. After thirty-two years' service it appeared inevitable that she would follow her many sister ships to that unhappy fate. However, for once it was not to be, for behind the scenes a number of interested parties were seeking to preserve for posterity what was then one of the few remaining examples of a Second World War warship. A joint committee representing the Imperial War

Museum, the National Maritime Museum and the Ministry of Defence started a study on the feasibility of such a project.

The result was the setting up in 1971 of the *Belfast* Trust, under the chairmanship of Sir Basil Giles. The necessary funds having been raised, the project was set in motion that autumn when the *Belfast* was towed to Tilbury for docking. Between 3 September and 14 October she was fitted out as a museum ship and on the latter date was undocked and towed up the Thames, through Tower Bridge, which she only just cleared, to her final and permanent resting place at Hays Wharf opposite the Tower of London. In 1972 her location, which ensured the maximum visitor footfall of any preserved ship, saw more than 550,000 people visit her, a higher total than the *Cutty Sark* or the *Victory*.

Here she has remained for a further forty years becoming part of the London Tourist scene with great success. The *Belfast* remains one of the major tourist attractions on London's visitor list and although many think her commercialism is overdone, it is considered necessary to keep such a large ship in reasonable condition. Long may she remain so.

WELLINGTON

The *Wellington* is moored at King's Reach by the Temple Stairs on the Victoria Embankment in London. She is the Headquarters ship of the Honourable Company of Master Mariners and has occupied this berth since December 1948.

The *Wellington* was built at Devonport Dockyard as a *Leith* class sloop, being laid down on 25 September 1933 and launched on 29 May 1934. She was accepted into the Royal Navy and commissioned at Devonport on 22 January 1935 and assigned for duties on the New Zealand Station, which was an appropriate choice for a ship of her name. At this period the Royal New Zealand Navy had little or no fleet of its own and a small squadron of ships from the Royal Navy was stationed in those waters.

The *Wellington* was of 990-tons displacement with engines developing 2,000hp (horse power) which gave her a maximum speed of 16.5 knots. She was designed as a surface escort for anti-submarine work with convoys and this speed was expected to be sufficient against the submarine types of her day. Her main armament was modest and, on outbreak of war in 1939, consisted of two single 11.938cm (4.7-inch) guns and a 7.62cm (3-inch) anti-aircraft gun.

After her first commission she re-commissioned at Wellington, New Zealand, on 26 August 1937 and the outbreak of war in Europe found her temporarily attached to the China Station. The need for convoy escorts in the North and South Atlantic was, however, paramount, and in

The impressive profile of HQS *Wellington*. (Copyright and Courtesy of The Honourable Company of Master Mariners)

November *Wellington* sailed for Freetown, Sierra Leone, for duty as ocean convoy escort.

In 1940 she was moved to home waters to escort coastal convoys around the shores of the United Kingdom and in June of that year, she was sent to le Havre to evacuate British troops during Operation CYCLE, which was the less well-known follow up evacuation from Operation DYNAMO from Dunkirk. She completed this mission on 9 and 10 June and then resumed her more routine duties on the convoy routes.

The rest of the war was spent in carrying out day-in-day-out convoy escort work, and this unspectacular but essential service kept her fully employed and, although *Wellington* herself attacked several U-boats and engaged enemy aircraft on numerous occasions, she was never credited with a 'kill'. However, she was most successful in her protective role and on three separate instances she carried out valuable rescue work. On 1 October 1940, the independently routed *Highland Patriot* was torpedoed and *Wellington* picked up the survivors and she performed similar duties when the same fate overtook the *Baron Lovat* on 7 June 1941 in Convoy OG 63 and the *Lavington Court* on 19 February 1942 with Convoy OS 34.

When the tide of war turned towards the end of 1942, the *Wellington* was one of the escorts involved in protecting the vast troop convoys which landed the British and American armies on the North African coast in November of that year, Operation TORCH. She was refitted during 1943 and her 7.62cm (3-inch) gun was taken out and replaced by much more efficient 20mm Oerlikon AA guns, of which she was fitted with six. In this manner she again returned to the Atlantic convoy battle working once more from Freetown. A further refit at Bermuda took place in mid-1944 and she then joined the Gibraltar Escort Force on 8 January 1945, where she remained for the rest of the war.

Upon the German surrender all the U-boats still at sea were ordered to surface, hoist black flags and surrender themselves to Allied warships and the *Wellington* was thus employed after VE Day in escorting such defeated enemy submarines into Gibraltar. In June she sailed for Plymouth where she paid off, being placed in Reserve at Milford Haven in August. Here she lay, along with scores of her contemporaries, awaiting her last voyage to the breakers' yard, but before she met this melancholy fate, the Honourable Company of Master Mariners stepped in.

Strange as it may seem for one of the oldest of man's professions, the Company was only founded in 1926 and is thus one of the more junior in the City. Whereas the great Livery Companies had flourished for centuries the Mariners, with traditions as ancient as any of the more senior Companies, had no Guild to represent them. This was not due to any lack of desire for such a Guild but because the very calling of the sea meant that it was extremely difficult for enough interested people to assemble at one time to organise its foundation.

After the First World War more positive steps were at last taken. At the Annual Shipmasters' Dinner in Liverpool in 1921, Sir Robert Burton-Chadwick made the suggestion that the profession was certainly capable of forming such a Guild or Company and he suggested the formation of The Worshipful Company of Shipmasters or something similar. The idea was enthusiastically received and, following intensive research in London and backing from many seamen, the Company of Master Mariners was duly formed on 25 June 1926.

On its foundation the Company limited itself to a membership of 500 and within eighteen months this total had been filled and a waiting list for membership was established. In March 1928, the then Prince of Wales, later King Edward VIII, and Duke of Windsor, became the first Master of the Company and in June of that year King George V bestowed the title 'Honourable' upon the Company. In August 1930 the King granted the Company his Royal Charter. In 1932 came the final step when the Court of Aldermen of the City of London conferred upon the Company the honour of Livery; this was the first time for over 200 years that a new Company had been so admitted.

The Company administers its affairs under the control of the Court, which consists of the Master, twelve Wardens and thirty-six Assistants. The only

Midships detail of the HQS *Wellington* October 2011. (World Copyright Peter C. Smith)

qualification for membership is that any Master Mariner of British nationality is eligible, providing he is the holder of a Certificate of Competency Foreign Going for not less than five years.

From its very beginning the Company felt the need for its own Hall but the various proposals mooted between 1926 and 1939 came to naught. After the war there seemed little likelihood of constructing a Hall in the City and it was therefore a welcome opportunity when, in 1947, the Admiralty made available for purchase one of the ships of the reserve fleet. The *Wellington* was selected as being in excellent condition and suitable for conversion and the Court decided to buy her with money subscribed by the Members and to convert her to the Company's floating Hall

and headquarters. It could have hardly been a more appropriate choice. The actual purchase was made on 25 June 1947 and permission was received to moor her in King's Reach. It is interesting to note that, technically therefore, the *Wellington* herself lay just *outside* the boundary of the City of London, the twin Griffins which guard the City limits being positioned just astern of her on the Embankment.

Wellington was towed to Chatham dockyard where extensive modifications were made to her, the cost being met from funds from an appeal launched by the Company, to which Lloyd's, the various shipping companies and others all responded. The conversion completed, the *Wellington* was towed to her berth on London's river and the small sloop which had spent so much of her service guarding the men of the Merchant Navy now became a fitting symbol of that service.

The ship is not open to the general public and the author considers himself very fortunate to have been taken round her from stem to stern. In addition to the various offices concerned with the Company's day to day administration, the *Wellington* contains many fine features appropriate to her particular role.

Her engine room is now a finely panelled Court Room with a raised dais towards the stern for the Master and Wardens. In the entrance lobby to the Hall there is a fascinating inlaid table reputed to have once belonged to Lord Nelson. On it, in a glass case, are the three volumes of the Roll of Honour to the members of the Merchant Navy and Fishing Fleets who lost their lives in the Second World War. Astern there is a smaller Smoker Room where the members meet.

To lead to the upper decks there is an ornate staircase which came from a Clyde packet and, among the display stands containing models of liners, cargo vessels and Chinese junks, it is interesting to note that the old hammock hooks are still in existence, a memento of a style of living now unknown in the Navy.

Also in the fore part of the ship there is a fine Model Room which leads to the Library. Here is contained a wide range of volumes on Naval lore and Maritime history.

Not all the offices on board the *Wellington* are utilised by the Company for also aboard are the headquarters of the British Ship Adoption Society. During the Second World War various towns 'adopted' fighting ships as their own and sent them comforts and mail. Much the same tradition is carried on by the Society today but they serve an educational function. They establish links between ships, both Mercantile, and, in recent years, Naval, and schools up and down the country.

The Society was begun as an experiment in 1934 when a London ship-owning company allowed four of its ships to be adopted by London schools with the voluntary co-operation of the masters of the ships. Such was the enthusiasm on both sides that in 1936 the Society was formed on a National basis to link ship-owners, masters and crews with the schools and pupils. Today the Society has some 670 ships and schools associated with it and its Committee of Management consists of representatives of ship-owners, officers and ratings, organisations, educational authorities, teachers' associations, The Geographical Association, The Royal Geographical Society and Government Departments.

The prime object of the Society remains to encourage the association of schools, colleges and kindred institutions with ships and those who man them. Visits are exchanged whenever the ships are in port. It is a strictly non-political and voluntary society and an annual subscription is paid by member schools. In some cases this is paid by Local Authorities who sponsor the schools' membership. Ship-owners and organisations which wish to encourage and help the work pay an annual subscription and today support from the ship-owners is the Society's chief source of revenue. In addition, gifts and donations are welcomed from friends of the Society. Combining as it does education with personal links of lasting friendship between the children and the men who keep the nation supplied, the Society's work is of national significance.

PRESIDENT

The *President*, along with her former sister ship *Chrysanthemum* which used to be berthed adjacent to her for many years but has now sadly gone, is a sloop whose design dates back to just before the First World War. Although many nations had built or were building submarines, they were not then a tried and tested weapon, although Admiral Jackie Fisher was farsighted enough to predict a great future for them. He was a rarity, however, and at this period the range of early submarines was very small and they were looked upon as a coastal defence weapon in the main, rather than the ocean-going menace they quickly became. It took a farsighted person like Fisher to foresee just how quickly the submarine would be developed under the pressure of wartime expediency but there was a realisation that some form of specialised warship would be required to combat it.

In the Royal Navy at that time the main preoccupation was to build up the main fleet, the battleships, battle-cruisers, cruisers of all types and destroyer flotillas in the face of the more obvious threat from the growing German Navy financed by the Kaiser's soaring ambitions. What money was available for other projects had therefore to be thinly spread and when the design of the Flower-group sloops was taken in hand they were required to fulfil several general-purpose roles rather than one specification.

The mine danger was seen to be a more pressing threat than the submarine and these ships were built as minesweeping vessels first and foremost but with refinements that made them also suitable for anti-submarine work, as fleet tenders, target vessels and other similar mundane, but essential, tasks. To facilitate delivery, these ships, although warships, were not built to the rigorous Admiralty standards but to the rather less exacting ones of Lloyds so that they could be constructed in shipyards not skilled enough to handle the more specialised Admiralty contracts and would not therefore tie up skilled labour which was needed elsewhere on more vital ship construction work.

They were not required to have speed which meant that they could be fitted with simple single-screw reciprocating machinery. Here again two immediate advantages resulted; the skilled labour force required to produce the high-speed destroyer turbines was not utilised and the ships themselves, once in service, could be run and maintained by the reservist engineers without any additional training. The first twelve ships of the Flower class proved most successful and repeat orders were given by the Admiralty throughout the war.

The submarine, in German hands, quickly moved from being a small, clumsy instrument of coast defence to the more serious threat of a long-range marauder which preyed upon defenceless merchant shipping and it was soon clear that nothing had been prepared to combat this type of warfare. The threat to reduce Britain by simple starvation was a real one. The adoption of the convoy system was very tardily implemented and to protect these large assemblies of merchant ships moving at slow speeds, huge numbers of escort warships were required. So serious did the problem become that large numbers of destroyers, so vital for work with the Grand Fleet and at Dover, were taken away for this new duty.

A lot of publicity was given to the very few successes achieved by disguised merchant ships, the 'Q' ships, or Decoy ships, which were given a concealed armament and lured the U-boats into gun range before opening fire. After a few months of this the German submarine commanders usually stayed below the surface and torpedoed their quarry but at least this had the advantage, from the British point of view, of limiting the number of attacks. It was with this concept in mind that the ninth order for Flower-class sloops was made. They utilised the same basic hull and machinery as the earlier sloops but their superstructure was rebuilt to resemble small merchant vessels with dummy deckhouse and false sides, behind which were concealed their guns.

The *Chrysanthemum* was one such vessel, being launched on 10 November 1917 by Armstrong's of Newcastle and the *Saxifrage*, belonging to the *Anchusa* sub-classification group, was another, being launched by Lobnitz of Renfrew on 29 January 1918. Both mounted two single 10.2cm

(4-inch) guns hidden below the bridge structure port and starboard and two 12-pounder guns hidden in a well aft. A similar deck well forward contained a depth charge mortar. The *Chrysanthemum* also had a kite balloon for spotting duties and two 45.72cm (18-inch) torpedo-tubes. There proved no use for the latter, however, and they were soon removed. These ships were around 1,290 tons, with overall lengths of 79.3m (262ft 3in), a 11m (35ft) beam and a draught of 3.51m (1ft 6in), and were good for about 16 knots.

On completion the *Saxifrage* was sent to the Western Approaches and the *Chrysanthemum* went out to the Mediterranean for convoy work. In the remaining months of the war both ships engaged German submarines but did not succeed

The forward deckhouse, open-air deck and bridge of HMS *President* moored on the River Thames. (World Copyright Peter C. Smith)

Bow view HMS *President* moored on the River Thames. (World Copyright Peter C. Smith)

in sinking them. After the Armistice in November, the *Saxifrage* was laid up in readiness for scrapping as being surplus to post-war requirements but the *Chrysanthemum* was utilised in yet another of her roles, that of fleet target tug and photography ship for the Mediterranean Fleet and continued in service until 1938. During this service she was accidentally holed by a 38.1cm (15-inch) practice projectile fired from the battleship *Queen Elizabeth*.

The Royal Naval Reserve had maintained a drill ship on the Thames for many years and by tradition the vessels allocated for this duty were named *President* after the President of the Privy Council. However, the name was much older. During the First Dutch War the second ship of the name had taken part in the battles of Portland, Gabbard and Scheveningen, all in 1653. She had been a 4th-rate of 445 tons and was commanded by Captain Graves. The third ship of the name was a frigate, formerly the French *Presidente*, which had been captured in the Bay of Biscay in 1806. She was of 1,152 tons, carried 38 guns and had a crew of 284. She was broken up in 1815.

The next *President* had been a 58-gun frigate of the American Navy, taken as a prize in 1815. In 1829 a new frigate was built to which the name was given and at the end of her useful service days, she was allocated to the Thames Division of the RNR and became a drill ship in 1862. In March 1903 she was renamed as the *Old President* and soon scrapped, while the Victorian Doterel-class sloop *Gannet* replaced her in May and was thereupon renamed as *President* to serve the newly created Royal Navy Volunteer Reserve. She reverted to sea-going duties in 1911 and another old gunboat, formerly the training ship at Blackfriars, the *Buzzard*, became the *President*. She had reached the end of her usefulness in 1919 (after seeing some war-related duty and then with The Marine Society) and the sloop *Marjoram* of the Flower class was selected as her replacement. She was, however, wrecked while under tow to London and a hurried search for a similar vessel resulted in the *Saxifrage* being saved from the scrapyard to become the present *President* on 9 September 1921, mooring at King's Reach from 19 June1922. It was a singularly opportune choice for the flower saxifrage is, of course, better known as London Pride. She was joined by her sister, the *Chrysanthemum* in 1938, when extra accommodation was required and she became a drill ship for the RNR. During the Second World War *President* provided training for Defensively Equipped Merchant Ship (DEMS) gunners, while naval recruiting utilised the *Chrysanthemum*, but they both reverted to their former duty post-war and remained commissioned Royal Navy war-ships for several decades.

Both vessels were painted in the old livery of black hulls, white upperworks and buff funnels and masts, which presented a Victorian appear-ance to London's riverside at Temple Gardens. They were given periodic refits when the masts and funnel were lowered and they were towed downriver to the docks. Apart from these isolated excursions they remained alongside the Embank-ment. The Ministry of Defence sounded their death knell when it transferred the 370-strong London Division of the RNR, the largest in the UK, ashore at the former P&O ferry terminal in St Katherine's Dock. Worse, they withdrew the protection that neither ship was ever to be scrapped, leaving them very vulnerable.

Sadly the *Chrysanthemum* did not survive the change and, after being sold to private owners, the *InterAction* Group, in 1988, was scrapped on the Medway in September 1995 despite protests as it was said she could not be made seaworthy. A mite of consolation may be had in that parts of her are being incorporated in the rebuilding of the *Medway Queen*. In April 2006 the *President* was purchased by MLS Business Centres Group plc, a serviced office organisation. In 2010 *President* underwent a large-scale renovation and was custom converted to become a prestige location conference and special occasion floating venue and has on-board offices for media world groups. As such she has numerous on-board venues including a 2,300 square feet Ballroom capable of holding 350 guests; the Gunroom service bar; the President Suite incorporating the Wrennery for eighty guests; the 120 guest Ward Room; the Board Room for twenty delegates, two open air decks, the Quarterdeck and the Front Deck with fabulous views of central London and the River Bar.

Hopefully then, her immediate future is assured and she is still listed on the National Register of Historic Vessels.

CUTTY SARK

The great days of the famed China tea clippers were brief; in fact they lasted only from the repeal of the Navigation Laws in 1849 until twenty years later when the Suez Canal was opened, but in that short space of time some of the world's loveliest and fastest sail-powered craft were constructed. These small vessels were built especially for speed and for the task of bringing home the cargoes of tea from China to the markets of London. The rivalry between such famous vessels as the *Ariel, Leander* and *Taeping* came about by the award of a premium of ten shillings (50p) a ton which was paid for the first cargo to arrive in England. In addition, the winning captain received a £100 bonus. The great annual races that took place were for the legendary 'Blue Riband of the Sea', awarded for the fastest passage. Nowadays this is awarded to the fastest Atlantic crossing by a passenger liner but in the mid-1800s it was the clippers that fought for this honour.

Perhaps the most famous race of all during this period was that which took place between the *Ariel* and *Taeping* in 1866. Both vessels sailed with the same tide from Foochow on 30 May and, after more than three months hard sailing across the South China Sea, across the Indian Ocean and round the Cape, they were seen off the Lizard, still together, on 5 September. The *Ariel* arrived in the Downs next morning at 8 a.m. with the *Taeping* ten minutes astern after a passage of ninety-nine days. These great days were almost drawing to a close when the *Thermopylae*, often described as the most magnificent of the clippers, was built at Aberdeen in 1868. On her maiden voyage she covered the distance from London to Melbourne in a time of sixty days, a feat which has never been equalled by sailing craft.

It was this vessel that the *Cutty Sark* was specifically designed to beat when she was laid down at the yard of Scott and Linton at Dumbarton. She was designed by Linton for John Willis, a Scottish-born London shipowner whose one burning ambition was to win the Tea Race. Accordingly, he demanded the very best of everything for his vessel in design, construction and materials. Despite this he had a Scot's eye for economics and the contract was an extremely tight one, being £17 per ton. The *Cutty Sark* when completed had a tonnage of 963 with a length overall of 280ft (85.34m) and a beam of 36ft (10.97m). She carried a sail area of 2,972.89m^2 (32,000ft^2) which gave her a speed of some 17 knots. The contract proved too much for the small Scottish shipyard which went bankrupt during her construction and she had to be finished off by another firm, Denny Brothers, also at Dumbarton. She was launched and towed from the Clyde to Greenock for fitting out and sailed from London on her maiden voyage on 16 February 1870, bound for Shanghai.

The name *Cutty Sark* itself, derived from the famous poem by Robbie Burns, where the witch Nannie, clad only in a chemise of Paisley linen, a 'cutty sark' (this translates into English as 'girl's shirt'), pursued Tam O'Shanter over the bridge at Doon running like the wind. It was a particularly apt name for a lithe sea-witch built for the greatest speed the wind could provide.

The *Cutty Sark* herself only made eight voyages home to London from Shanghai or Woosung with cargoes of tea between 1870 and 1877. Her first voyage was one of her best, 109 days from Shanghai to Beachy Head, and the following year she clipped a single day from this, but, even so it was far from an outstanding performance, for although her masters were brilliant seamen, not all of them had the drive to force the ship and her crew to the utmost limit.

15

The strikingly beautiful lines of the *Cutty Sark* in her dock at Greenwich in 1974. (World Copyright 1974 Peter C. Smith)

Her only trial against her rival the *Thermopylae* almost ended in complete disaster. This was in 1872 when both ships left Woosung fully laden on the same day and when they passed into the Indian Ocean the *Thermopylae* had a very slight lead. In the ensuing month, however, the *Cutty Sark* forged ahead and it was estimated that she had established a lead of about 643.747km (400 miles) when she ran into a heavy gale and lost her rudder. Despite terrible conditions which persisted for a week, repairs were effected on board and a jury rudder was built and fixed, but the week lost was decisive and the total journey time of 120 days was bettered by a week by the *Thermopylae* but never again were ships destined to race from China in comparable conditions.

With the growing predominance of steam power, the *Cutty Sark* was hard put to it to find cargo in the years which followed, and during the early 1880s sought what general cargo she could find in Far Eastern waters. It was not until 1883 that she again found regular employment, being utilised on the Australian wool route. Her first passage in this period was one of her finest performances for she took a mere eighty-two days from Newcastle, New South Wales to Deal along the notorious Cape Horn route through the 'Roaring Forties' in atrocious weather conditions. With the appointment of the dynamic Captain Woodget in 1885, the *Cutty Sark* really excelled herself and time and time again was the first home.

Her most remarkable performance was turned in during 1887–8, when she made the passage from Newcastle, NSW to Deal in the time of seventy-three days and she finally had the satisfaction of consistently beating the *Thermopylae*'s time year after year. Despite this, the *Cutty Sark* eventually proved too uneconomic to run and in 1896 she was sold to the Portuguese.

She was renamed as the *Feirrira* and served the Portuguese company of J. A. Ferrira for almost a quarter of a century, surviving the Great War and plying her slim hull to the Cape and the West Indies with general cargo. In 1920 she was again renamed as *Maria do Amparo* on a change of ownership and underwent a long refit in London.

Bow view and mastings, showing the *Cutty Sark* at Greenwich, south-east London, after her refurbishment which cost £50m and included the controversial raising of the vessel over eleven feet above her berth. Visitors can examine her hull from below and the surround contains a state of the art corporate venue and café. Inside the ship herself, people can roam around the decks, enjoying an all-new interactive museum. (World Copyright 2012–2013 Peter C. Smith)

Port bow view of the restored and rebuilt *Cutty Sark*. The encasing of the ship means that her fine lines cannot be viewed externally. (World Copyright 2012–2013 Peter C. Smith)

Here fate took a hand, for, while sheltering in Falmouth harbour from a storm, she was seen by Captain Walter Dowman, who had known and loved her in his youth. So determined was he to save the *Cutty Sark* that he there and then opened negotiations for her purchase. Sold to him for £3,750 at Lisbon, a tug was sent to tow her home. Here Captain Dowman carefully re-rigged her as a clipper, for she had been much cut down. He cherished her until his death in 1936, whereupon his widow presented her to the Thames Nautical Training College and, in 1938, she was towed to Greenhithe on what was to be her last sea voyage. At Greenhithe she joined another old-timer, the former HMS *Worcester*.

Both veterans lay undisturbed by the Second World War but, with the building of a new steel training ship in 1949, both became surplus to the requirements of the College. The *Worcester*, sadly, went to the breakers' yard but a happier fate awaited the *Cutty Sark*. She was offered to the National Maritime Museum, but they had neither the resources nor the authority to maintain her. The then Director of the museum, Frank Carr, approached the old London County Council. Thanks to their enthusiastic response the *Cutty Sark* was moored off Greenwich for the 1951 Festival of Britain and money was allocated for her docking. In 1952 the *Cutty Sark* Preservation Society was formed under the auspices of His

Royal Highness The Duke of Edinburgh, who had long been enthusiastic about the ship. The LCC provided space at Greenwich and, in December 1954, the *Cutty Sark*, fully restored to her former splendour, was moved into a specially constructed dock.

The ship was formally opened to the public at a ceremony performed by Her Majesty Queen Elizabeth II on 25 June 1957. Since that time many millions of people have visited her. However, there still remained a great deal of painstaking research before the *Cutty Sark* could be presented as she was in the 1870s for no plans existed but, gradually, piece by piece, the evidence was compiled which enabled the authentic rigging and decoration to be emplaced.

As well as the ship herself, visitors were able to see aboard her a fine collection of merchant ship figureheads from the private collection of John Sidney Cumbers of Gravesend and various models and exhibits telling the story of the China Clippers and the tea trade. On the practical side the *Cutty Sark* was utilised for evening classes for yachtsmen. In 1972 the Maritime Trust took over the ship on behalf of the Society and she became one exhibition of the National Historical Fleet, Core Collection. She is now recognised as a Grade I Listed Monument.

An ambitious multi-million renovation programme, currently estimated at a staggering £46 million, was initiated in 2006 which involved raising the ship up three metres so she could be viewed from below, incorporating an art museum. The hull of the *Cutty Sark* was to be supported by a steel belt with a new steel reinforced keel and steel strutting and incorporating a glass enclosed lift leading to the weather deck. Not everyone felt that this would maintain the ship in her authentic state.

Great damage was done to the central section of the vessel by a fire on 21 May 2007, which subsequent detailed examinations by London Fire Brigade, the Metropolitan Police, Forensic Science Services and Dr Burgoyne's & Partners jointly concluded was caused by an industrial vacuum cleaner being used as part of the renovation work, that had inadvertently been left switched on for forty-eight hours before the fire started. Fortunately, due to the conservation work, many original artefacts, including her masts and the ship's saloon, had already been removed to a storage facility and were safe.

Restoration work was resumed and the wooden planks from the ship's hull were among many original features to be restored. On 10 December the work had reached the final stages and a crane lowered into place the ship's foremast, with the other two masts following over the next two days. She was officially re-opened by HM The Queen in her Diamond Jubilee year in April 2012.

GIPSY MOTH IV

The story of this famous little vessel was initially the story of the courage and determination of one man, Sir Francis Chichester. Always an adventurer in the best sense of the word, Francis Chichester was born in Devonshire and, at the age of eighteen, left his native shores for New Zealand.

His war service was spent as a navigation instructor and, post-war, he turned his business eye toward map publishing in London. His purchase of the 13-ton *Gipsy Moth III* resulted in the fastest single-handed crossing of the Atlantic and he repeated his exploit in 1964. During this race, his experiments with a radio telephone link had proved successful and, with this in mind, Chichester then embarked on the planning of his most audacious self-imposed challenge yet, a solo round-the-world circumnavigation in an attempt to equal the best speeds of the old clipper ships. To achieve this, Chichester required and received a great amount of sponsorship for the voyage. And so it was that the *Gipsy Moth IV* came to be designed. The name originated with the Gypsy Moth light aircraft which Chichester had flown, and three earlier yachts.

The design team of John Illingworth and Angus Primrose at Emsworth in Hampshire was given the task of producing a craft which could be handled by one man and be capable of sailing to Sydney in 100 days. This proved to be a tough assignment, for the two requirements were not necessarily compatible. A ketch rig was adopted for ease of handling and the mainsail had an area of 289ft^2 (26.85m^2), which was the maximum Chichester felt he could operate alone. In all, the total sail area for *Gipsy Moth IV* was 854ft^2 (79.34m^2).

The ratio of length to beam was 16m (54ft) overall and 11.8m (38½ft) at the waterline, with a 3.2m (10.5ft) beam which showed a bias towards the speed requirement. A novel feature which was to prove its worth was the Blondie Hasler self-steering gear. This, briefly, consisted of an elongated servo blade which was connected to a wind sail at the stern of the yacht where it was clamped edge to the wind. Should the *Gipsy Moth IV* have veered off her pre-set course the wind pressure on the sail would have twisted the servo blade and the water pressure swung it sideways. The action operated a pulley system connected to the main rudder and brought *Gipsy Moth IV* back on to course.

In construction also, the *Gipsy Moth IV* incorporated revolutionary new ideas and concepts for that period, which are now, many decades on, normal and routine, but which then were trail-blazing. She was built in the famous Gosport yard of Messrs Camper and Nicholson and was the first such vessel in which they utilised the cold-moulded method of construction using Honduras mahogany. By this method an accurate mould was made and the keel stern and sternpost were constructed as a single item. The hull itself was then built up using six layers of thin veneers which gave it a completely watertight form of high accuracy. The mould was then removed and the decks fitted. The final stage was the completion of the cabins and cockpit. The total cost of the *Gipsy Moth IV* when completed was £35,000 and she was launched by Sheila Chichester on 8 March 1966.

Trials completed, the *Gipsy Moth IV* took part in a farewell ceremony at Greenwich in the shadow of the *Cutty Sark* whose feats along the wool route she hoped to emulate. This done, Chichester took her to Plymouth and, on Saturday 27 August 1966, she crossed the start line, destination Sydney, New South Wales.

The last glimpse of land came a week later when *Gipsy Moth IV* passed Madeira and for the next 19,312.128 kilometres (12,000 miles) Chichester would only have his radio and the isolated contact with passing shipping to keep him in touch with the rest of the world. With no communications satellites and other modern technology which makes this feat so easy today, Chichester was very much reliant on his own skill and endurance. Eighty days out and the *Gipsy Moth IV* was going well but, on 15 November, while in the lonely southern stretches of the Indian Ocean, a period of severe gales wrecked the self-steering gear. Not admitting defeat, Chichester set up a jury rig by utilising the staysail and continued his voyage undaunted, but he had lost several precious days and all hopes of keeping to his 100-day timetable were lost.

Still it was to a well-deserved and outstanding welcome that *Gipsy Moth IV* arrived at Sydney, 107 days out of Plymouth, a total distance of some 22,128.48km (13,750 miles). Although Chichester was weary from his long voyage, he was determined to continue with his aim of returning to England via Cape Horn, but first some essential repairs and modifications had to be made to his craft in the light of his experience on the outward journey. Accordingly, the self-steering device was repaired and strengthened and two steel plates 2.133m (7.5ft) long were bolted to the keel to give increased stability.

Refreshed in himself and with a seaworthy vessel under his feet once again, Chichester set out on his return leg on Sunday 20 January 1967. But now he sailed as *Sir* Francis, for this honour had been bestowed upon him by Her Majesty Queen Elizabeth II in recognition of his achievement and pluck on the outward leg of his journey. Soon after leaving Sydney harbour, the

The *Gipsy Moth IV* back in action and good as new thanks to the work of Eileen Skinner and Rob Thompson who bought her in October 2010 and are establishing the *Gipsy Moth* Trust as a Charity to ensure her future. (UK Sailing Academy via Eileen Skinner)

Gipsy Moth IV almost capsized when she was struck by a large wave, but she righted herself and continued on to the north of New Zealand and then on into the 'Roaring Forties'. Here a succession of gales in this notorious area of the southern ocean quickly sped the *Gipsy Moth IV* on toward Cape Horn and what many considered to be the most dangerous part of the entire voyage. The Horn had an evil reputation in the days of sail, many a fine vessel ending her days on its barren shore. Sir Francis took it in his stride and was found by the Royal Navy Ice Patrol Ship HMS *Protector*, making a good 8 knots in a Force 7 gale. Good fortune favoured him through the South Atlantic and he crossed the equator on 24 April, but then became becalmed south-west of the Azores.

Despite this setback, Sir Francis expected to reach Plymouth on Sunday 28 May at 11 a.m. Still

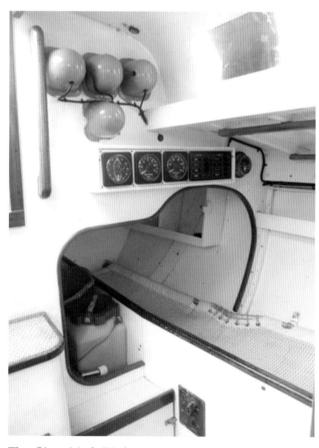

The *Gipsy Moth IV* showing internal storage area and fitments. (Copyright and Courtesy of Eileen Skinner)

airs meant, in fact, that it was late afternoon before *Gipsy Moth IV* was first sighted by the crowd of a quarter of a million people who had assembled on the shore at Plymouth and the Hoe. An armada of 1,000 small vessels met him some distance out and salutes of sirens and whistles were added to the firing of cannon as he stepped ashore at the Yacht Club steps to be welcomed by the Lord Mayor and the Royal Navy's Commander-in-Chief, Plymouth. He had made the then fastest circumnavigation achieved by any small vessel; by sailing 24,140.16km (15,000 miles) non-stop he had broken that record too and in fact had sailed twice the distance achieved by single-handed voyaging and by sailing 2,300km (1,400 miles) in just eight days had broken the speed record also.

This, however, was a mere prelude to the great home-coming that Sir Francis and *Gipsy Moth IV* were to receive when they reached the Thames and London. On 7 July, at Greenwich Royal Navy College, Her Majesty Queen Elizabeth II knighted him in the Grand Square, using for the ceremony the sword with which Queen Elizabeth I had knighted Francis Drake on his return from his own round-the-world voyage in the *Golden Hinde* in 1581. The *Gipsy Moth IV* was then sailed upstream where Sir Francis and Lady Chichester attended a civic banquet at the Mansion House given in his honour by the Lord Mayor with all the awe-inspiring pomp and ceremony that only the City of London can provide. The *Gipsy Moth IV* was later sailed round to Bucklers Hard on the Beaulieu River where Lord Montagu of Beaulieu organised yet another great reception in the Master Builder's House.

The *Gipsy Moth IV* was herself placed on exhibition at the Boat Show at Earls Court and it was here that the leader of what was then the Greater London Council, Sir Desmond Plummer, announced that Lord Dulverton had presented her as a gift to London, that this offer had been welcomed and that she would be preserved in a specially constructed dock at Greenwich close by the famous *Cutty Sark* that had served as her inspiration. And so it was that, on 10 July 1968, she was first opened to the public in her new home. Sir Francis died on 26 August 1972 and

The Maritime Trust took over the *Gipsy Moth IV* as well as the *Cutty Sark* and installed her in her own small dry-dock at Greenwich. She achieved a very high footfall in the Capital, but, down the decades, this had an adverse affect on her structure and she finally had to be closed to the public. Even so a steady deterioration occurred and in 2003 the *Yachting Monthly* editor, Paul Gelder, campaigned to have her restored and more, to take place in another circumnavigation to

Looking forward along the deck from the cockpit of the renovated *Gipsy Moth IV* (Copyright and Courtesy of Eileen Skinner)

commemorate the 40th Anniversary of her famous voyage.

The following year the *Gipsy Moth IV* was bought by the United Kingdom Sailing Academy for £1m and a gin-and-tonic (Sir Francis Chichester's favourite tipple) and sent back to Camper & Nicholson's Gosport yard, where she was restored at a cost of £300,000. Renovated once more, and with a full crew this time under Richard Bagget, with Dewi Thomas as First Mate, Paul Gelder as crew leader and Matthew Pakes, Peter Heggie and Elaine Cadwell as initial crew members, on 25 September 2005 she set off from Plymouth Sound to participate in the 2005–07 Blue Water Round the World Rally. At first things went splendidly, but, on 20 April 2006, *Gipsy Moth IV* was run on to a coral reef at Rangiroa, Tuomotus in the Pacific, some 320km (200 miles) from Tahiti and badly damaged.

Salvage work was conducted and she was towed to Tahiti and loaded on to a ship for passage to Auckland, New Zealand, where she was repaired. By 23 June 2006 she was back in commission and ready for the homeward leg via Australia, Singapore, the Indian Ocean, the Suez Canal and Gibraltar. She once again reached Plymouth after a voyage of 45,486 km (28,264 miles) on 28 May 2007, being greeted by Giles Chichester, son of Sir Francis. Her voyage was commemorated in a book but *Gipsy Moth IV* herself was put up for sale at Lymington Marina at a price of £250,000. She was finally purchased in October 2010 by Rob Thompson and Eileen Skinner, who launched the Gipsy Moth Trust on 21 July 2011. This Trust has the stated intention of putting her on permanent display at Cowes, Isle of Wight, as well as sailing her in various yachting events around the UK.

GOLDEN HINDE

The word *Hind* in English has always meant a female red deer (*Cervus Elaphus*) and nothing else. The *Golden Hind*, which was Drake's flagship was not originally thus named, being built as the *Pelican* and only re-named midway through her circumnavigation of the globe. She was a 'race-built' galleon, by which was meant she had lower superstructure and smaller guns, but with longer ranges, than the conventional Spanish type, which made the English ships faster and more handy. Whether the word was spelt *Hind* or (as is the current fashion) *Hinde*, it was certainly as *Hind* that a 28-gun ship was built in 1545 and sold ten years later, and so is likely that her successor's name was so spelt in 1577. Drake's naming of his vessel was in deference to his principal sponsor of the voyage, Sir Christopher Hatton, who had a golden hind as part of the family coat of arms, but, in retrospect the *Golden* may either be taken to refer to that particularly attractive shading of the deer's normal pelt, as portrayed in her figure-head, or to the fact that looted Spanish treasure had indeed turned Drake's vessel golden, whatever one's fancy! The name of the current replica is used here nonetheless as it is her we are describing. Some may well question her inclusion in these pages at all as there is nothing original about her, but I felt her worthy as she is a carefully constructed copy of one of the most famous of English ships whose ancestor's deeds were outstanding in laying the very roots of our rich maritime legacy.

The original *Golden Hind* was, as noted, built as the *Pelican* at the Tudor dockyard at Aldeburgh, Suffolk, where another of his ships, the *Greyhound*, was also constructed. The dockyard and much of the old town has since been swallowed up by the sea but Pelican Cottage still exists there and can be visited. In 1576 she moved to Coxside,

Plymouth. She was a wooden-built, three-masted vessel carrying five square sails on her two forward masts and a triangular fore-and-aft rigged lateen sail on her after mast. This gave her a total sail area of around 386m^2 (4,159ft^2). These could give her a best speed of around 8 knots (14km/h). She had an overall length of 36.6m (120ft) and a beam of 6.1m (20ft), with a 4.1m (13.5ft) draught and displacing 300 tons. She was armed with two peteras (small cannon) on her fore deck and two more on her poop deck aft. For long range fire, something the English excelled in, there were two falcons (2-pounder cannon) on the fo'c'sle and two in her stern, while for close-range broadside pounding she had fourteen minions (4-pounders) on her main gun deck. She had a crew of twenty officers and sixty seamen.

The little English ships that made that historic first circumnavigating the globe were similarly mere cockleshells and with the *Pelican* were the *Marigold*, the *Elizabeth*, the *Swan* and the tiny 15-ton *Christopher*. Drake had with him aboard his flagship his brother Thomas, nephew John and a cousin, young William Hawkins. These worthies were not officers as we know the term today but horny-handed seamen or gentlemen adventurers seeking fame and fortune, and it was not always a happy mix. Drake summarily dealt with any rival, like Thomas Doughty, in a drumhead court martial midway through the voyage, thus laying the basis in maritime law that it is the Captain rather than the Lord who is in charge at sea.

After a false start the squadron finally got underway from Plymouth on 13 December 1577. It took six months to reach Port Julian off the South American coast where on 20 June Doughty's execution took place, the *Christopher* and *Swan* were demolished and the *Pelican* became *Golden Hind*, despite the fact that re-naming a ship in mid-voyage was considered 'unlucky'. Drake, however, was a man who made his own luck. The fact that Doughty had been Hatton's personal secretary may possibly have made Drake think that by thus renaming the ship in honour of the Hatton crest it might act as some sort of atone-ment for his beheading of Doughty, who had been his sponsor's friend and confidant, but this was never made clear. The remaining trio of ships then penetrated the treacherous Straits of Magellan and reached the Pacific Ocean on 6 September 1578, but in those notoriously stormy seas the

The *Golden Hinde* replica in St Overie Dock at Cathedral Street, Bankside, Southwark. (World Copyright Peter C. Smith)

Marigold herself foundered on 30 September while the remaining pair were blown back to Cape Horn and separated on 7 October, *Elizabeth* returning to England alone after waiting a while, but Drake pressed on alone with the whole of the Spanish Empire open to his marauding. He duly made the most of his opportunity, raiding Valparaiso on 5 December 1578 and taking a Spanish treasure ship. Following a refit Drake moved on and his next prize was the Spanish galleon *Nuestra Señora de la Concepcíon* (*Our Lady of the Immaculate Conception*, (allegedly irreverently nicknamed *Cagafuego* by her crew) on 1 March, from which his haul was 80lb of gold, thirteen chests of pieces of eight, 26 tons of silver and jewels. After sailing north as far as the present site of Vancouver, Canada, the *Golden Hind* turned back to replenish in New Albion (at present-day Drake's Bay, Marin County, just north of San Francisco, California) before heading out into the Pacific on 23 July, arriving in the Philippines on 16 October and the Spice Islands on 3 November. Calling at Java the *Golden Hind* continued under sail until she anchored at Sierra Leone on the west coast of Africa on 22 July. *Golden Hind* of the original five-ship squadron returned in triumph to England on 26 September 1580, after a voyage that had lasted for 1,017 days.

For his services to the English Crown (both official and unofficial!) Good Queen Bess knighted Francis Drake on the ship's deck on his return home, She visited the *Golden Hind* which was moored in the Thames at Deptford dock, decorated with flags and bunting and dined aboard her. No doubt the estimated £600,000 (approximately £25 million in today's money) treasure he brought home influenced her somewhat.

But the enmity that existed between Catholic Spain and England soon saw outright hostilities between them with the despatch of the huge Spanish Armada by which Philip hoped to crush the upstart island. He got a drubbing for his pains, and it was another *Golden Hind*, a 50-gun pinnace commanded by Thomas Fleming, that first glimpsed the enemy fleet off the Lizard on 19 July 1588 and brought the news back to Plymouth of the approach of the Spanish, where

Drake took the tidings in his famous imperturbable way before setting about defeating it.

Drake's *Golden Hind* had been put on public display in dock at Deptford at the Queen's behest, and was subsequently laid up as a monument 'for all time', but she slowly rotted away over the course of a century. It was not until recent years that a seriously organised search was initiated to discover her remains on the original site at Convoys Wharf, but the whole area is up for re-development for housing so she may well be lost for eternity. Meanwhile, upstream her replica flourishes.

In 1934 a half-size replica existed and today there are *two* full-size replicas. One was built for a television series. She cost £25,000 and was later moored at Brixham, Devon as a permanent exhibition ship. She is open to visitors throughout the summer months and at select times in the

The crow's nest, rigging and mast aboard the *Golden Hinde* replica at St Overie Dock at Cathedral Street, Bankside, Southwark. (World Copyright Peter C Smith)

winter. She hosts a series of educational seminars and has frequently featured on television. Contact address for her is The Quay, Brixham, Devon, TQ5 8AW or at drake@goldenhind.co.uk.

The second and most authentic and well-known is the full-size replica that was lovingly hand-built in Devon as an educational ship for the Crowley Maritime Corporation of San Francisco, California, with the financial backing of West Coast shipping magnate Tom Crowley at a cost of $1.5 million. She was designed from the start by naval architect L. Christian Xorgaard to be fully operational. The builders were J. Hinks & Son Shipyard, Watertown, Appledore and, when she was launched a decade later, she was as faithful a reproduction as is likely to be had and was a fully seaworthy vessel. Of course the Tudor builders had no plans but this vessel used every available clue from contemporary illustrations, to descriptions plus reference to the known methods of the time. She has five oak decks sealed with oakum and is packed with authentic copies of the internal artefacts of the period. She was laid down on 30 September 1971 and launched by the Countess of Devon on 5 April 1973 who broke a bottle of mead on her bows.

In fact, this replica has actually outdone her famous forebear in sea miles sailed and has covered some 225,000 km (140,000 miles) in total, which is the equivalent of *five* circumnavigations of the earth. During the course of these voyages she has called at more than 300 ports all over the world and been visited by several million visitors, an incredible record of achievement well worthy of her namesake. She visited several British ports in 1973, including London itself, and then commenced her first ocean-spanning journey in 1974 when she was sailed to San Francisco in commemoration of the original voyage. Under command of skipper Adrian Small, she berthed at

Pier 41 South, close to Fisherman's Wharf. Here she was first opened to the public as a museum ship and later appeared in the film *Swashbuckler*.

In 1979 she sailed to Japan via Hawaii thus crossing the Pacific, and was used to 'star' in the film *Shogun*, in which she played the part of the *Erasmus*. With another film in the can, entitled *Drake's Venture*, she left for the United Kingdom via Hong Kong thus completing her first round-the-world passage. Between 1980 and 1985 she again toured the United Kingdom and then sailed via the Caribbean to Vancouver in which she featured during the Expo 86 trade fair. Under joint owners Roddy Coleman and John Carter she then made her way down the west coast of the USA visiting sixty harbours in the states of Washington, Oregon, California and Texas and then, with her service support vessel the *Elizabeth* (the *Sea Surveyor*) made a similar progression up the eastern seaboard from Port Lavaca, Texas up through Baton Rouge, Louisiana, New Orleans, Key West, Miami Cape Canaveral and so on between 1989 and 1990, before returning to London. Here she 'starred' in another film, *St Trinian's 2*.

Since 1996 this *Golden Hinde* has had a semi-permanent berth in the St Overie Dock at Cathedral Street, Bankside, Southwark, in the shadow of Southwark Cathedral itself and the site of Clink Street prison and the equally renowned Globe Theatre. Here she is open to the public and hosts tours, corporate entertainments and conferences, and many school groups who participate in appropriate costumes of the first Queen Elizabeth's reign.

Contact The *Golden Hinde* Trust, Office and Souvenir Shop, 1 & 2 Pickfords Wharf, Clink Street, London SE1 9DG. Nearest Tube/Station – London Bridge. Tel – 020 7403 0123. info@goldne hinde.com

CAVALIER

The destroyer became probably the best-known warship type of all in the twentieth century. A totally British innovation through and through, the first of them took to the water just before the end of the nineteenth century in fact and were then, and remained, the fastest warships afloat, a position they maintained for many decades. In fact the present *Cavalier* took part in the last speed competition held by the Royal Navy when she challenged the *Rapid* to a duel in July 1971 and just beat her. The earliest craft were painted black which reflected their then intended role as night-time attackers of heavier ships and, with their lean and dashing appearance, they made an immediate appeal to the ship lover, which they retained until the late 1940s when the series of beautiful ships was brought to an abrupt termination by the arrival of such raggedly and ugly vessels as the Weapons and Daring classes.

The destroyers' innumerable exploits in two world wars added to an already unrivalled reputation for dash and skill in the face of odds and

The last conventional Royal Navy destroyer still remaining, HMS *Cavalier*, was paid off in July 1972 and the author was the only historian invited to attend her last voyage up the Medway. Comparison of photographs I took then, and again almost forty years later in 2011, reveal just how well she has been preserved. The *Cavalier* proceeding up the Medway in July 1972. (World Copyright 1972 and 2012 Peter C. Smith)

The commanding officer of HMS *Cavalier*, Commander Goddard, on the bridge with his First Lieutenant in July 1972. (World Copyright 1972 and 2012 Peter C. Smith)

such destroyer names as the *Shark* and *Nestor* at the Battle of Jutland, and the *Cossack* and *Kelly* in the second great conflict, made the destroyers household names. They were originally built to act as defenders of the battle fleets from the threat of torpedo attack by the swarms of torpedo boats built by rival powers like France and Russia in the late 1880s. Admiral Jackie Fisher went to Alfred Yarrow, who already had a unrivalled reputation for building high-speed craft, and asked him to provide a ship fast enough to catch the enemy torpedo boats, and yet carry an heavy enough armament to sink them when they were so caught. The result was the little *Havock*, which joined the fleet in 1893 and soon proved herself ideal for the job in hand. She was followed by a large programme of 'torpedo-boat destroyers' or TBDs as they were originally termed and, over the next two decades, the type, soon abbreviated to just 'destroyer', grew steadily in size and power but still remained the fastest vessels afloat in any navy.

In the First World War they fulfilled the traditional role of defence against enemy torpedo boats but they had also been so developed that they were able to take over the torpedo boat's role in a sea-going capacity and to attack the enemy battle line. The duties of anti-submarine escort and high-speed minelayer were also added at this time and the destroyer emerged as one of the most ubiquitous warships of the fleet by 1919. During the Second World War, although their numbers had been stupidly reduced by political cut-backs and appeasement of our potential enemies, they still were called upon to land and evacuate troops from Norway, Dunkirk and Crete, to provide anti-aircraft protection for convoys and to perform as fast minesweepers in addition to all their other duties.

Post-1945, however, the rapid decline of the main fleets increasingly left the conventional destroyer type with no role to fulfil and her place as a general-purpose warship in the modern fleet has been taken over by the enlarged frigates, which, although much slower and less-heavily armed, are better designed for anti-submarine work which came to be considered the main threat during the Cold War period. Although the classification 'Destroyer' continued to be retained for a limited construction and indeed still is, after the Daring class of the early 1950s such ships more resembled cruisers in size, appearance and mission and had little or no connection to the classic destroyer. Thus, by 1972, only two true destroyers were left afloat, the sister ships *Caprice* and *Cavalier*, and of this pair only *Cavalier* was a fully operational unit, the *Caprice* being utilised at Plymouth in a purely training capacity. If *Cavalier*

at that time was not the last destroyer, as was claimed by the Press, she certainly is now!

The *Cavalier* herself was one of the almost 100 War Emergency destroyers; she was of the CA Class and was laid down in 28 March 1943 at the shipyards of J. Samuel White at Cowes, IOW. She was launched on 7 April 1944 and completed on 22 November that same year. Her displacement was 1,170 tons and she carried an armament of four single 11.43cm (4.5-inch) guns, two 40mm Bofors and six 20mm Oerlikon anti-aircraft weapons along with eight 53.34cm (21-inch) torpedo tubes and depth-charges. She joined the 6th Destroyer Flotilla, Home Fleet, at Scapa Flow carrying the

The *Cavalier* in October 2011, preserved at Chatham in No. 2 dry-dock, the same dock in which the *Victory* was built. (World Copyright 2012 Peter C. Smith)

That same ship's bridge aboard the *Cavalier* in October 2011, with the Captain's chair raised on blocks just as it was forty years earlier. (World Copyright 2012 Peter C. Smith)

pendant number R73 (which later was changed to D73 which she still nominally holds).

From January to May 1945 the *Cavalier* took part in the final maritime operations in European waters, which included service in February as escort for one of the last Arctic convoys to the Soviet Union, for which she received a Battle Honour; air/sea strikes against German shipping targets off the coast of Norway and rescue missions of Norwegian civilians during the German evacuation. On completion of these duties the ships of the 6th Flotilla were refitted in readiness to join the British Pacific Fleet in the planned final assault on mainland Japan, Operation OLYMPIC, but, with the dropping of the atomic bombs, the war in the east came to an abrupt conclusion

before *Cavalier* reached the area, but she was employed in a warlike operation in the Dutch East Indies when she bombarded Surabaya in Java to put down a rebellion of native government troops against the Dutch and the following year she helped quell a mutiny in the Royal Indian Navy at Bombay (currently Mumbai) in February. She returned home in 1946 and in May was placed into reserve at Portsmouth, where this author first saw her as a young boy, and where she remained idle until 1955.

At this latter date it was decided to modernise the eight CA class destroyers and employ them for further active service and *Cavalier* was thus taken in hand at J. I. Thorneycroft's shipyard in Southampton. This refit lasted until 1957 and, on

15 July that year, she was commissioned to replace the *Comus* in the 8th Destroyer Squadron (an American term now imposed on the Royal Navy to replace the respected ancient and traditional term Flotilla), again in the Far East. In December 1962 she embarked 180 soldiers at Singapore and ran them to Brunei at high speed to quash rebellious forces. She continued to serve in Far Eastern waters until 1964, visiting Australia, Japan, Korea and El Salvador. During the confrontation with the brutal Sukharno dictatorship of Indonesia she was active with the fleet protecting Borneo.

The *Cavalier* was again placed in reserve on completion of these duties, respectively at Chatham, Devonport and Gibraltar for long periods, before once more sailing to the Far East on her third tour of duty in that part of the world. In 1970 the epic race between *Cavalier* and another War Emergency destroyer (albeit one that had been reduced to a frigate many years earlier), the *Rapid*, took place, which *Cavalier* won at 31.9 knots by a distance of just 27m (30 yards). In 1966 she was employed on the Beira patrol blockading the then rebellious state of Rhodesia, before going to the Mediterranean. Her armament was, by now, much modified and, in its final state, consisted of three 11.43cm (4.5-inch) guns, two Bofors, a triple-barrelled Squid anti-submarine mortar and a Seacat missile system.

Her final period of operations began in 1970 at Portsmouth, under the command of Commander C. A. Snell RN. She was employed mainly in coastal waters with the occasional visits to the Channel Islands, Norway and the Netherlands and took spells of duty with the fishery protection patrols off Iceland. Her last commander, who joined her in July 1971, was Commander P. M. Goddard RN, who had flown in the rear seat of the winning Phantom aircraft in the 1969 Transatlantic Air Race.

It was then that the media took up the story that, when *Cavalier* finally paid off into reserve in July 1972, the last of the true destroyers would have vanished from the Royal Navy. This news received much attention in the press and an appeal was launched to save her for posterity. Back then some remnant of pride in the Royal Navy's

history was still apparent and, in conjunction with the Maritime Trust, a *Cavalier* Trust was set up and it was estimated that £60,000 would be needed to preserve her from the scrapyard and turn her into a floating museum. The Chairman of the *Cavalier* Appeal was Rear Admiral Douglas Parker and the original hope was to moor *Cavalier* at Southampton, where she was expected to be a great attraction.

It was at this date that the author, on account of his various books on destroyers and destroyer history, briefly became associated with the *Cavalier* as he was lucky enough, thanks to the kindness of Commander Goddard, to receive an invitation to sail on the *Cavalier* during her last voyage up the Medway in July 1972. Representing *Navy International* magazine, with representatives of the press and one of her former Commanding Officers, we were taken out from Chatham dockyard by an Admiralty tug into the Thames Estuary off Sheerness. A distant speck on the horizon soon manifested itself as the *Cavalier* steaming at high speed to meet us. She certainly did not look or act her twenty-seven years for she overtook our scurrying tug with contemptuous ease and performed a selection of complicated turns and circles for the benefit of the cameramen, myself included. I was told that spare parts to keep her in operation were very hard to obtain but, despite this, she was still capable of 31 knots when the average speed of the new surface fleet had shrunk to a mere 25 knots.

When we finally boarded her, Midshipman Robert Wilkey from Bristol took me on an extended tour of the ship, from bow to stern, and the workings of the armament, radar and engine room were patiently explained in detail. The *Cavalier* was one of the last warships in the Royal Navy in which hammocks were slung in the traditional manner. A Royal Marine Band was playing on the jetty when she finally arrived at Chatham and rang off engines for the final time. It was a very moving occasion.

Unhappily in the years that followed that first flush of hope, things did not work out as hoped and *Cavalier* was shunted from port to port, gradually deteriorating as the years passed. The problem was always visitor footfall sufficient to maintain her upkeep. These Emergency Destroyers were just that, built *en masse* and in a hurry for the duration of war, and keeping her slender plates in seaworthy condition required money. Back in reserve at Portsmouth once more, Lord Louis Mountbatten lent his name to the campaign to raise the £65,000 required and after five years the destroyer was handed over to the Trust on Trafalgar Day 1977, with a special dispensation (likewise granted to the *Belfast*) of being able to

True destroyers were built for speed, as the knife-edge bows and beautiful lines of the last conventional such vessel in the Royal Navy illustrate perfectly. (World Copyright 2012 Peter C. Smith)

continue flying the White Ensign and to continue using the designation HMS although no longer a commissioned warship.

In August 1982 *Cavalier* officially opened as a museum ship at Southampton, but the expected

visitors failed to materialise, Southampton always being a mercantile, rather than a naval port. When the new marina was opened at Brighton, along the coast, it was thought this might prove a more suitable venue and *Cavalier* was duly moved

The addition of the Seacat AA missile tower ruined her perfect destroyer lines but it ensured that she continued in front-line service until the early 1970s when most of her contemporaries had long gone to the scrapyards. HMS *Cavalier* at Chatham Historic Dockyard, October 2011. (World Copyright 2012 Peter C. Smith)

thither in October 1983, but this also failed to draw people to her. Even more remote was her next billet, on the River Tyne in north-east England to where she was shuttled off in 1987 as part of a planned Maritime Museum for South Tyneside Metropolitan Borough Council. Instead of a proud exhibit, she was allowed to fall into a rusting, listing derelict, isolated in a dry dock. Her fate seemed irresolvable but there were those with stout hearts determined to save her even now and in 1998 the re-invigorated *Cavalier* Trust bought her back and she was towed south to her true home, Chatham Dockyard, once more, where her post-RN service had started so many years earlier. She was docked once more, this time in the No. 2 dry dock, famous for building HMS *Victory* and became part of the Chatham Historic Dockyard display.

More recently a committee decided on how a tribute to Second World War destroyers should be incorporated. This author's own submitted idea, for a glass screen with the silhouettes of each of the British destroyers sunk in the Second World War with the destroyer's name inscribed below,

to be placed alongside her berth, similar to the USAAF Memorial at Duxford IWM, was given short shrift, even though popular with many of the actual destroyer men themselves. Instead, the evacuation of troops from Dunkirk and Crete was commemorated, although these events, worthy enough as they were, formed a mere fraction of the destroyers' widespread and normal duties in two world wars. However, at least *Cavalier* herself should now survive, after many years of being shunted around the country from port to port, homeless and neglected. Chatham was her home port so it is appropriate she should end her days there.

I visited her again in October 2011 and I was given the freedom to explore her. It seemed strange to reflect that almost forty years had passed since I last trod her decks and that she had been an elderly lady even then. Little or nothing had changed, and *Cavalier* was again in fine condition, a real credit to Chatham Historical Dockyard and those who run her. Long, long may she remain to remind the nation that once, not too long ago, we really had a Navy.

GANNET

The ships that have carried the name *Gannet* in the Royal Navy have all been small craft. The first was a 16-gun brig built in 1800 and the second was an 18-gun sloop built at Lynn in 1814 and sold out of service in 1838. Then came another sloop and finally the *Gannet* which has survived down the years in a number of guises to the present day.

She is a valuable contribution to the story of the Royal Navy for she represents perfectly the transition period of the mid-Victorian Navy. Originally *Gannet* was designed with a two-cylinder engine and two boilers and carried three masts. She was fitted with a propeller which was raised to reduce drag when sailing under sail alone, and her single funnel was telescopic so that it could be lowered

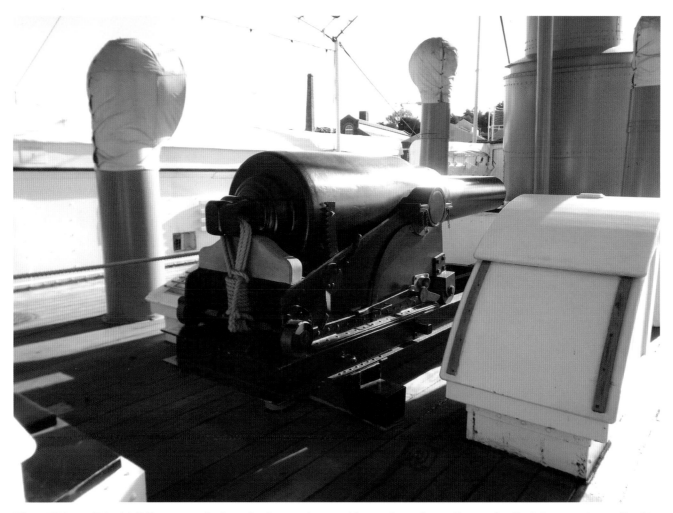

The 17.78cm (7-inch) B.L. upper-deck swivel gun along with cowls and ventilators for Red Sea service at Suakin aboard HMS *Gannet*. (World Copyright 2012 Peter C. Smith)

in order to avoid getting in the way of the sails. She was, therefore, what was known in the service as an 'up-funnel, down-screw' sloop. These composite sloops were designed to patrol all over the world to police the more distant stations and islands of the Empire and the sea routes, upholding the 'Pax Britannica' wherever there was enough liquid for a Royal Navy warship to float.

She was 51.816m (170ft) long by 10.972m (36ft) broad with a draught of 4.572m (15ft) fully laden.

Bow view HMS *Gannet* shows a conventional hull, cut away to allow her traversing deck gun to fire ahead on either the port or starboard bow. Her two anchors are stowed astern of the cut-aways to prevent interference with the guns, a necessary compromise. (World Copyright 2012 Peter C. Smith)

She was built at Sheerness Dockyard and was launched on 31 August 1878. Her armament consisted of two 17.78cm (7-inch) breech-loading guns mounted on swivelling mounts and four 64-pounder breech loading guns mounted on swivelling platforms. She had a tonnage of 1,230. She was re-armed and re-rigged in the 1890s and served before that at Suakin, a Red Sea port, in 1887. She had a teak hull and was originally rigged as a barque. Her hull below the waterline

Upper deck detail from the port bow showing ship's funnel and masting arrangement, with gun ports and the multi-barrelled light weapons which she carried to police the remoter areas of the Empire.
(World Copyright 2012 Peter C. Smith)

is copper sheathed and was found to still be in excellent condition on examination a century later.

She remained in the Royal Navy from 1878 until 1903 when she became HMS *President* as described earlier. On completion of these duties in 1913 she was laid up in the Hamble river where she served as the Training Ship *Mercury*. Under the command of Commander C. B. Fry, she served as the dormitory ship for 120 boys undergoing training for the Royal and Merchant Navies and she remained in this capacity for over fifty years, not finally going out of service until 1967. She lay for a time moored off Whale Island in Portsmouth Harbour awaiting an Admiralty decision with regard to her ultimate disposal, being under the care of Commander Kearsley of the *Belfast*. It was then that the Maritime Trust stepped in and took her over from the Ministry of Defence.

Mr Jack Hayward generously donated £100,000 toward her reconstruction and long-term hopes were that she would find herself a permanent berth on the Thames in the old St Katherine's Dock near Tower Bridge. Instead, she has become part of the Chatham Historic Dockyard collection. She was extensively surveyed during a dry-docking at Southampton in 1972 and was found to be in near perfect condition underwater so that very little work was at that time required. It was also fortunate that the original builders' drawing from Chatham still existed as they greatly facilitated her reconstruction.

Gannet is among the very best of the restored mid-Victorian warships and is thus historically very important.

OCELOT

The submarine *Ocelot* (S17) is now preserved at Chatham Dockyard and is in very good condition. She belonged to the one of last classes of Royal Navy submarines to be powered by conventional diesel-electric engines, only the *Upholder* class succeeding them before all building was concentrated on nuclear-powered vessels. The Oberon class comprised thirteen which were built for British service, the *Oberon, Ocelot, Odin, Onslaught, Onyx, Orpheus, Olympus, Opossum, Opportune, Oracle, Osiris, Otter* and *Otus*, while several more were either built for, or transferred to, other navies including Australia, Brazil, Canada and Chile.

This attack/patrol submarine was of the twenty-seven strong *Oberon* Class, and a sister ship to the *Onyx* also described in this book, and she

The massive conning tower of the submarine HMS *Ocelot* on exhibition at Chatham Historic Dockyard in October 2011. She was one of the last conventionally-powered submarines built for the Royal Navy and among the most silent of her kind. (World Copyright 2012 Peter C. Smith)

was actually originally ordered for the Royal Canadian Navy. *Ocelot* (S17) belonged to the second improved group of this class and was the last one to be completed. She was built on No. 7 Slip at Chatham Dockyard, and was the very last

submarine to be built here, being laid down on 17 November 1960, launched on 5 May 1962 and first commissioned on 31 January 1964. Like her sisters the *Ocelot* was built of glass fibre and alloy, the only such British submarine class to utilise

The bulbous nose housing her sensors and her six torpedo-tubes give the British submarine HMS *Ocelot*, on exhibition at Chatham Historic Dockyard in October 2011, a menacing appearance. She was one of the last conventionally-powered submarines built for the Royal Navy and among the most silent of her kind. (World Copyright 2012 Peter C. Smith)

these materials. She was of 1,610 tons standard, 2,030 tons surfaced displacement, and 2,410 tons submerged displacement, with an overall length of 88.5m (295ft 25in), 73.456m (241ft) between parallels, a beam of 8.1m (26.5ft) and a 5.5m (18ft) draught. She was powered by two Admiralty Standard Range 1, supercharged 16VMS–ASR1 Diesel and two electric engines developing 3,680hp each, driving two shafts which gave her a high submerged speed of 17 knots and a surface speed

The limited space aboard submarines of the conventional type, of which HMS *Ocelot* on exhibition at Chatham Historic Dockyard in October 2011, was one of the last to be built. (World Copyright 2012 Peter C. Smith)

of just 12 knots. She had a range of 19,170km (10,350 nautical miles) and could dive to a depth of 200m (650ft).

The *Ocelot* was armed with eight 533.4m (21-inch) torpedo-tubes, six in the bow for Mark 24 wire-guided Tigerfish attack homing torpedoes and Mark 8 torpedoes, a design dating back to 1928 with an improved warhead from 1943; plus two short tubes as anti-submarine defence weapons in the stern.

The Marconi-built Mark 24 Tigerfish torpedo was fitted with an acoustic seeker in its nose and was wire-guided, both the *Ocelot* and the *Tigerfish* being equipped with the necessary wire dispensers. Data was downloaded from the submarine weapon control station to the torpedo's onboard computer. The Tigerfish warhead was the 134kg PBXN 105 warhead from the BAe Royal Ordnance Division. When the torpedo neared the target, a magnetic proximity fuse and an impact fuse detonated the warhead. The speed of this formidable underwater weapon was 25 knots in passive mode but 35 to 50 knots in active seeker mode. The maximum range of the Tigerfish was 40 kilometres.

An alternative payload for *Ocelot* was up to fifty mines. She also carried Type 1002 Surface Search and Navigation radar, a Type 187 Active-Passive attack Sonar set and a Type 2007 Long-Range passive Sonar set plus MEL Manta UAL or UA4 radar warning outfits and decoys. She later deployed the submarine version of the Harpoon guided weapon. Her complement was seven officers and sixty-two men.

Ocelot joined the 3rd Submarine Squadron at HM Naval Base Clyde, at Faslane. With her diesel motors charging her batteries she could slip through the depths almost noiselessly employing her electric motors. The class were famous for their engine and equipment soundproofing which lent itself to particularly silent running which made them difficult to detect. *Ocelot*, like her companions, was deployed throughout the Cold War on surveillance and intelligence-gathering duties, garnering information about the enormous submarine fleet of the Soviet Union and patrolling off their bases like Murmansk. During her first three commissions, *Ocelot* racked up in excess of 144,840.96km (90,000 miles). Conditions aboard were arduous but tales of not being able to wash or change clothes for a week or more are 'old salts' yarns' as the *Ocelot* was equipped with a distiller which meant frequent washing was possible and later a reverse osmosis machine was fitted which also helped.

In common with other conventional submarines, the government of the day decided to scrap them all and *Ocelot* was sold in 1992. Chatham Royal Dockyard had closed and become Chatham Historic Dockyard with the waning of British naval power and they acquired *Ocelot* which enabled her to permanently return to her roots where she had commenced being built thirty years earlier. When I inspected her in November 2011 I was the only visitor and was thus given a very personal and thorough viewing. She is in excellent condition throughout as the accompanying photographs clearly show

Ticketed tours by the very helpful, experienced knowledgeable and patient volunteer guides are available at the Historic Dockyard, Chatham, Kent, ME4 4TZ, Tel: 01634 823800. Fax 01634 823801.

MEDWAY QUEEN

The famous old *Medway Queen* is one of the most illustrious of the paddle steamers to be saved for the nation. She was built in 1924 by the Ailsa Shipbuilding Company at Troon on the River Clyde in Scotland for the New Medway Steam Packet Company of Rochester, Kent. Steel hulled and with a gross tonnage of 316, she had a length of 54.559m (179ft) 9in, a beam of 7.315m (24ft), and 12.192m (40ft) across her twin paddle-boxes. She carried two cylinder compound engines built by Ailsa and a three furnace Scotch type boiler, which was originally coal-fired but was converted to oil firing in 1938.

From her first season in 1924 until her final withdrawal from service on 8 September 1963, a period of just under forty years, the *Medway Queen*, with the exception only of the war years, plied as a pleasure steamer on the River Medway and the Thames Estuary. She proved a popular vessel in service and her years were largely uneventful until, with the coming of the war in 1939, the Royal Navy took her over. She was requisitioned because her shallow draught made her, and her sisters, ideal ships for minesweeping work and it was for this function that she was converted. She was strengthened and fitted with minesweeping davits and sweeps wires and given a defensive armament of an old 12-pounder gun dating from the First World War. In such condition she was commissioned in November 1939 as HMS *Medway Queen*, and sailed to war following a short working-up period.

She joined the 10th Minesweeping Flotilla at Dover in January 1940 and, with eight similar vessels so converted, swept the Straits of Dover through the bitter winter of that year, being successful in bringing to the surface a few mines. Minesweeping is wearisome and monotonous work at best, with the ships sailing before dawn to sweep up and down the channels day in and day out, the boredom only on rare occasions at this stage of the war being broken by any hint of the enemy. All this was to abruptly change, however, when the German Army overran France and the Low Countries in a brief campaign in May and June 1940. The British Expeditionary Force (BEF), caught up in the collapse of their continental allies, fought its way back to the beaches around Dunkirk harbour and Admiral Ramsay and his staff at Dover, with considerable foresight and great improvisational skill, organised a vast armada of warships supplemented by all manner of light craft, to bring them safely home. The 10th Flotilla received orders on 27 May to proceed to the beaches north of Dunkirk and, during the following seven days, the *Medway Queen* made no less than seven trips to those beaches, enduring dive-bombing and shelling, to bring off over 7,000 troops, an individual total only exceeded by the destroyers and some larger merchant vessels. For this she became known as the 'Heroine of Dunkirk'.

After this epic she reverted to less hectic war duties and finished her period of Royal Navy service as a training ship. In the summer of 1947 she was returned to her owners having undertaken an extensive refit and once more took up her peaceful trade as a pleasure steamer on the Medway and the Thames. She was, in fact, the last of the Company's paddle steamers to pay off. Her second great occasion came in June 1953, when the Queen reviewed the Fleet at Spithead at the time of her Coronation. This great naval spectacle, the size of which was never again to be seen, was a memorable one and the *Medway Queen*, appropriately enough, was there as one of the excursion

The *Medway Queen* in 1974. It is hoped to have her fully rebuilt and moored at Gillingham, Kent, by 2011 and that she will steam again. (Copyright David L. Wright)

vessels that followed the Despatch Vessel *Surprise* with the Queen embarked, through the long ranks of assembled warships.

When the *Medway Queen* was finally withdrawn from service at the end of the summer season ten years later, the Paddle Steamer Preservation Society called a public meeting at which it was decided to set up the *Medway Queen* Trust. In spite of many vicissitudes, which twice brought the old vessel almost to the breakers' yards, the

46

Trust's sustained efforts enabled her to survive for over twenty months until she was bought by commercial interests.

In September 1965 she was towed from the Thames for the last time to become a floating club house and marine centre at Island Harbour on the Medina River, near Newport, Isle of Wight, where she remained for many years. With her tall funnel and flush deck typifying the traditional estuary paddle steamer which had dominated pleasure resorts for so many years, and with her outstanding war record, there was little doubt the *Medway Queen* was the finest candidate of her type for national preservation, both as a vessel of historic interest and a memorial to the epic work of the little ships at Dunkirk during Britain's darkest days. Eventually, she proved too small and was replaced by the *Ryde Queen* and quickly became derelict.

From this sad and sorry state she was again brought back from the brink in 1984 by a group of businessmen and returned to the Medway at Chatham for refitting. However, funds proved insufficient and she was again left to rot away on a mud bank. The following year another effort was made and the *Medway Queen* Preservation Society stepped in, purchasing the hulk for £15,000 and starting the long process of restoration at Damhead Creek, off the Medway. As the years followed, her condition further deteriorated, and she sank at her berth more than once and seemed irredeemable. Another last-minute reprieve followed with a grant of £1.87 million pounds made by the National Lottery Heritage Fund in 2006.

The rebuilding work on the *Medway Queen* – Starboard Bow. It shows the ship in July 2011 with side plating up to main deck level and the promenade deck structure visible to the left of the picture. The yellow horse shoe is one of the hydraulic riveting units. (Richard Halton reproduced by kind permission of *Medway Queen* Preservation Society)

With such a sum, salvation was again a possibility and she was taken round to Bristol for the work to commence. It was decided to do the job properly with the traditional riveted hull rather than welding being employed. While this major reconstruction was progressing the Preservation Society on the Medway called on the skills, time and love of numerous volunteers to refurbish various fixtures and fittings and the rebuilding of the ship's bridge. This work was aided by further international fundraising and in 2010 an additional funding for the second stage of the rebuild was received, under the 'Heroes 2C' project. The work continues steadily with the hope of final completion in 2012 and the further hope that she will once more sail the Medway and Thames as so often before.

At the time of writing, the project is moving ahead at a rapid pace with the deck planking fully restored in Kent and the apprentices, who will refit the ship in 2012, signing on. Restoration of the deck planking involved removal of a glass-fibre coating from the ship's time on the Isle of Wight and then removal of all nails, screws and bolts. Some 1,828.8m (6,000ft) of planking was found to be re-usable and was sawn and planed to consistent width and thickness. All holes were then plugged in readiness for the next stage. The planks were laminated onto new timber to restore the original thickness. This required use of a two-part, marine grade, epoxy resin. The laminated timber was clamped and kept for a minimum of twenty-four hours in a temperature-controlled poly-tunnel while the resin cured. Eight sections of wood, up to 6.09m (20ft) in length, were handled in each batch at the rate of three batches a week. Mike Johnston designed and installed an automatic electrical system which kept the temperature above 20°C for the curing process. Final machining prepared the timbers so that they are ready for installation on the completed hull.

At Bristol Yard the *Medway Queen* is really beginning to take shape and July 2011 saw a Heritage Progress meeting where the ship underwent her inspection for the 75 per cent complete stage. The engine cylinder block is in the process of being insulated before the engine re-assembly prior to putting the engine back into the ship. The galley has been put in place, sections of the promenade deck have been erected and work on the paddle shaft and wheels are well in hand. Replacement deck stanchions are now being manufactured and work will commence shortly on the windows. The plating of the hull plating continues apace. David Abels of the Albion Dockyard Ltd was quoted on the limited accessibility of the work thus: 'Inside bow plating – red hot rivet in one hand, backing tool in other hand, wedge in your third hand and a hammer in the fourth! All while lying on your side, at full stretch to reach into a stupidly small space.' The old ship's port-side paddle sponson brackets are in place and when both the paddle sponsons are added the ship really will start to look like her old self. You can follow this thread of the *Medway Queen*'s restoration on web cams at the MQPS web site www.medwayqueen.co.uk

The society's base has moved to its new location on Gillingham Pier whose address is: *Medway Queen* Preservation Society, Gillingham Pier, Pier Approach Road, Gillingham. ME7 1RX. When the vessel returns there, and once the displays in the new centre are complete, visitors will be most welcome. The workshops and apprentices focused on refitting the ship in all respects supported by a European Regional Development Fund (ERDF) grant. This grant, under the 'Interreg IVA 2 Seas' programme, has been made as part of the 'Heroes of the two seas & Heroes2Sea' project which brings together three restoration groups. The Medway Queen Preservation Society is working in close cooperation with the New Belgica Association and the Association Tourville to further their respective maritime heritage projects. The apprentice training is being conducted in association with Mid-Kent College and the restoration programme is being recorded by nine media students from the college under the guidance of Gregg McDonald of Consequential Films.

CAMBRIA

For over 200 years the Thames sailing barges were a common sight along the lower reaches of London's great river and also in the estuary of the Medway. They were unique and, although designed, for the larger part by rule of thumb, over the years as flat-bottomed bulk carriers for shallow rivers, they ventured as far afield as the Low Countries as well as being prominent on the coastal routes from the Thames to the Humber and round to Plymouth. The east coast ports of Great Yarmouth and King's Lynn also saw them as did the harbourmasters at Dunkirk and Boulogne and, on one notable occasion, no less than six went to South America.

Crewed only by a skipper and a mate, their cargo comprised anything and everything to anywhere from anyplace to the nation's capital city. Hay from the East Anglian farms to feed the thousands of London horses in the nineteenth century, bricks to build the sprawling metropolis wider yet from the Kentish brick kilns, and the trans-shipment of other cargoes from the Pool of London and the docks downriver to the customer. By the late 1800s there were more than 2,000 of these barges plying the Thames and coastwise trades, providing quick and cheap transport links. Indeed, the barge could often reach communities completely inaccessible to any other form of bulk cargo carrier, up isolated inlets and creeks, resting their broad bottoms on muddy estuaries and floating off again 'on a patch of dew' with the turn of the tide.

They were in continuous demand throughout the Great War but it was inevitable that the growth of the motor vehicle would see the decline of the barge. Gradually economics decided that it was better to carry goods direct from the docks to the customer by lorry rather than trans-ship to the barge. In the early twenties there were still more than 1,500 barges in use but by the 1939 this total had shrunk to around 600. The last Thames barge to be built was the *Cabby* in 1928. And so the distinctive spritsail barges with their ochre-coloured sails passed away until only the *Cambria* remained trading under sail in isolation, and it was she who was saved by the Maritime Trust to remind us of all of them.

Cambria was built by the famous Thames firm of F. T. Everard and Sons of Greenhithe. Established in 1889 by Frederick T. Eberhardt, his sons William and Frederick went to Great Yarmouth to apprentice as shipwrights and on their return they were each set to work to build a barge to his own standard. The results were the *Cambria* and the *Hibernia*, the former being built by William. Both vessels were launched in 1906 and the *Cambria* cost £1,895 against the *Hibernia's* £1,905 and both turned out to be identical in construction and appearance. *Cambria* had a length of some 27.736m (91ft) and a beam of 6.675m (21.9ft). Her gross tonnage was 109 and on her mainmast, topmast, mizzen and bowsprit she carried a total sail area of 5,000ft^2 (464.57m^2). She traded the coastal routes for over fifty years, doing well in the trade up to Great Yarmouth before she was eventually laid up in the 1960s when sail trading proved no longer viable. During this long lifespan she distinguished herself during the great races held for the barges on the Thames and the Medway, which have more recently been revived once more. The year she was built she came second in the Thames race while, in 1926, she was the winner of events, repeating this performance the following year and proudly flying her championship pennant.

The last skipper of the *Cambria* when she served under the Everard flag was Captain Bob Roberts, and when she became surplus to the Everard fleet, he was given, and promptly took, the chance

The Thames sailing barge *Cambria* (Copyright & Courtesy the *Cambria* Trust)

to take her over as her owner. Thus, while the majority of the Thames sailing barges were converted to houseboats, or were given auxiliary machinery, Bob Roberts and the *Cambria* con-

tinued to ply the broad river route into the heart of London with cargo carried by wind and tide alone for a further five years, from 1966 to 1971. She was by then over sixty years old and even

The main seating area below aboard the Thames sailing barge *Cambria*. (Mark & Cathy Chapman by permission of the Cambria Trust)

Bob Roberts could no longer keep her trading, but fortunately The Maritime Trust had been formed and they offered to buy her for preservation from the last of the 'sailormen' as the sailing barge skippers were known.

So the *Cambria* is still with us, the one unaltered surviving representative of the many thousands which thronged the Thames highway. As a memorial to the skippers and mates and the craftsmen who built, rigged and repaired them, the old *Cambria* is a worthy vessel. For many years she was moored at Rochester, by the old Castle, and it was hoped to ultimately find her a berth on the Thames itself, in the waters she had sailed so often, and knew so well. The *Cambria* Trust is now trying to raise £1 million to restore her totally and use her for sail training and educational purposes on the Thames, Medway and Swale. Contact Basil Brambleby, Secretary, *Cambria* Trust, 32 Pilgrims Way, Cuxton, Kent, ME2 1LG; mancyandbasil@talktalk.net

Thames sailing barges still afloat, and their locations, include

Name	Location	Name	Location
Adieu	St Katherine's Dock	*Kitty*	Maldon
Alice	Portsmouth Harbour	*Lady Daphne*	St Katherine's Dock
Ardaina	St Katherine's Dock	*Lady Jean*	Maldon
Beric	St Katherine's Dock	*Lady of the Lea*	Faversham
Blackthorne	River Alde	*Marjorie*	Hoo
Cabby	St Katherine's Dock	*Mirosa*	Faversham
Centaur	Maldon	*Montreal*	Battersea
Cygnet	Pin Mill, Harwich	*Nancy Grey*	Leigh-on-Sea
Dawn	Maldon	*Orinoco*	Faversham
Decima	Heybridge	*Phoenician*	St Katherine's Dock
Dinah	Pin Mill, Harwich	*Pudge*	Faversham
Edith May	Lower Halstow	*Reminder*	Maldon
Edne	St Osyth	*Reporter*	Faversham
Ena	Hoo	*Thistle*	Maldon
Ethel Ada	Lodon	*Tollesbury*	Faversham
Felix	St Katherine's Dock	*Victor*	Mistley
Greta	Whitstable	*Whippet*	Lower Upnor
Hope	Maldon	*Wyrenhoe*	Maldon
Hydrogen	Maldon	*Xylonite*	Wapping
Ironsides	Maldon		

KINGSWEAR CASTLE

In the late 1950s paddle steamers were still common and were to be found working from many coastal towns and resorts around our shores, but in the space of little more than a decade the paddle steamer became a rare sight indeed. With the growing realisation that they were gradually disappearing came action to save one or more of these vessels. In 1959 Alan Robinson was crossing from the Isle of Wight to Lymington on the paddle steamer *Freshwater* and learned that she too was destined to be sold out of service. He determined there and then upon the formation of a society dedicated to preserving one of these craft and, following letters to the press, the Paddle Steamer Preservation Society was formed that same year.

Immediate success followed and the society was instrumental in saving several of these famous old vessels from the scrapyard. Equally important was the fact that they managed to purchase one of the finest of them. This was the *Kingswear Castle* and it was the first time that a Society, as opposed to individuals, museums or public bodies, actually acquired a steamer of commercial size for such preservation.

The *Kingswear Castle* was built in 1924 by Philip and Son of Dartmouth. She was a steel-hulled vessel of 94 gross tons, with a length of 32.918m

The paddle steamer *Kingswear Castle* in classic pose. (Courtesy and Copyright of John Megoran Paddle Steamer *Kingswear Castle*)

(108ft), a beam of 5.334m (17.5ft) and a draught of 0.990m (3.25ft). She was powered by two two-cylinder compound diagonal engines, built by Cox and Company of Falmouth in 1940, and had a single furnace, a Scott-type boiler and was coal fired.

She was built for the River Dart Steamboat Company and the engines in fact came from one of their earlier vessels of the same name, built by Cox at Falmouth, which she replaced. Long and low in the water, with a single funnel behind the paddles, the *Kingswear Castle* is typical of the

Close-up detail of *Kingswear Castle*: stern decks and seating. (World Copyright 2012 Peter C. Smith)

long line of pleasure steamers which served on our navigable rivers for over a century, and she is thus an important addition to the vessels preserved in the country.

She served on the picturesque river Dart for forty years until she was displaced by diesel vessels and was withdrawn from service. She was laid up by the company at the end of the 1965 season and, when it became clear that she would not attract a purchaser for further commercial use, she was purchased by the Paddle Steamer Preservation Society, who, with limited resources, had been awaiting a paddle steamer of modest size to become available. In August 1967 she was taken under tow to the Isle of Wight, to be moored next to the paddle steamer *Medway Queen* and placed under the care of the Medway Queen Marina Company. There she remained for four years until events made it possible for the Society to set about serious restoration.

The *Kingswear Castle* was moved, again under tow, to the Medway where she arrived on 18 June 1971 and work was put in hand by members on a major overhaul and refit with the intention of making her the Society's flagship. Restoration was a considerable undertaking and the Society is therefore always eager to welcome new members able to contribute suitable skills and enthusiasm to conduct such important work. Apart from concerning themselves with all the aspects of paddle steamer preservation their activities range widely. Coastal pleasure steamers were chartered for cruises each year, and photography, research and exhibition work is undertaken. The aim was to return the *Kingswear Castle* to her former glory as an active, rather than a merely passive, example of our maritime past. She now operates on both the Medway and the Thames with regular cruises and special events in conjunction with the Paddle Steamer Preservation Society. Contact: Paddle Steamer *Kingswear Castle*, The Historic Dockyard, Chatham, Kent, ME4 4TQ. Tel: 01634 827648 or info@kingswearcastle.co.uk

VICTORY

This most famous of all ships of the Royal Navy was laid down as a first-rate ship of the line at Chatham Dockyard on 23 July 1759 during the Seven Years' War. Although destined to become the best known of them all, this vessel was, in fact, the seventh ship to bear the name *Victory*.

The first ship of the name was originally built as the *Christopher* in 1506, a 700-ton ship mounting fifty-two guns, which was later presented to Queen Elizabeth I and rebuilt. She fought the Spanish Armada in 1588 and continued to serve for 100 years. She was again rebuilt in 1603, becoming the *Royal Anne* before going to the breakers in 1606. She was followed, in 1620, by a 40-gun vessel, built at Deptford on the Thames. During the Dutch Wars she was present at the battles of Dover

The most famous warship in the world, Admiral Horatio Nelson's immortal HMS *Victory*, still a serving unit in the Royal Navy, undergoing her latest in a long line of restorations at Portsmouth Naval Dockyard, October 2011. (Copyright & Courtesy of Dawn and Sean Rayment)

(1652) and Portland, Gabbard and Scheveningen in the following year and was then reconstructed to emerge as a second-rate carrying eighty-two guns in 1666. In fact she was to all intents and purposes a brand new ship and qualifies for inclusion as the third *Victory*. She also saw much service and fought at the battles of Orfordness in 1666, Sole Bay in 1673 and at the battles of Schooneveld and Texel in 1673.

The next ship of the name was the former first-rate *Royal James*, a 100-gun vessel built at Portsmouth in 1675 and renamed in 1691. She fought at the battle of Barfleur in 1692 and then was rebuilt completely, emerging as the fifth *Victory* in 1695 but saw no further major actions. The sixth ship was another first-rate, also built at Portsmouth in 1737, but she was lost in 1744 and the name became available for new construction again.

The new ship was built as a flagship and had a length of 56.69m (186ft) and a beam of 17.32m (51ft 10in), and carried 100 guns. The ships of this period were in truth 'hearts of oak' for it has been calculated that the construction of the *Victory* took no less than 2,000 oak trees. Her massive gun armament was distributed over three decks and fired through ports cut in the 0.609m (2ft) thick sides of the ship. On the lower deck, just above the waterline, were ranged the largest cannon, fifteen 32-pounders along each side. The middle deck contained fourteen 24-pounders evenly distributed while, on her upper deck, quarter deck and forecastle she carried forty-two 12-pounders and two of the massive 68-pounder carronades. These latter were mounted on the bow and were designed to pound the ships of the enemy line during the close approach of the squadron. They fired a mixed shot and grape charge which could inflict appalling damage among the close-packed ranks of an opposing ship. Her displacement was 3,500 tons making her one of the largest vessels in the fleet. Her construction, however, was not hurried due to the successes of the Seven Years' War which left the country breathing space before the threat of France loomed up once more. She was not finally launched until May 1765, when she was floated out of the Old Single Dock at Chatham. The proud new vessel immediately

went into reserve, laid up 'in ordinary' as it was then termed, and here she remained in idleness for thirteen years.

It was in May 1778 that the *Victory* was commissioned for service for the first time, under the command of Rear Admiral Lindsay and she was fitted out for duties as the flagship of Admiral Keppel, commander of the Grand Fleet. In July of the same year she saw her first action, an indecisive clash during which the *Victory* suffered thirty-five casualties. In the two following years she remained in home waters wearing the flags of Admirals Hardy, Geary and Drake but saw no action. In 1781 Admiral Parker flew his flag in the *Victory* and he was succeeded by Rear Admiral Kempenfelt. Off Ushant in December he led his squadron against a large French fleet escorting a valuable convoy and the ensuing engagement resulted in the taking of fifteen French vessels without loss to the British of a single ship.

In 1792 Admiral Lord Howe took the *Victory* as his flagship and sailed with a fleet to relieve Gibraltar, which was besieged by the Spanish and blockaded by the large French fleet from Toulon. He was successful. *Victory* underwent a long refit between 1787 and 1790 at Portsmouth and, on completion, sailed with Admiral Lord Hood for duty in the Mediterranean, blockading Toulon after the expulsion of the British army from that port.

She remained in the Mediterranean for several years wearing the successive flags of Admirals Mann and Jervis. It was as flagship of the latter that she was heavily engaged during the great victory of the battle of Cape St Vincent in 1797 but, on her return to Chatham, she was reduced to duties as a hospital ship. Then, in 1800, she was taken in hand once more for a large rebuilding, which lasted for three years and, in May 1803, she hoisted Nelson's flag and sailed once more for Mediterranean waters to renew the fight with the French.

Here the Royal Navy was again enforcing the blockade of a French squadron at Toulon but, in an effort to lure the enemy out to sea and thus engage them, Nelson kept his main force back over the horizon. In January 1805 the French fleet under Admiral Villeneuve slipped out and headed westward through the Straits of Gibraltar. Their plan was to lure the Royal Navy to the West Indies and then to return secretly and, with the English Channel unguarded, to enable the invasion of England to take place without interference. On learning that the French ships had sailed,

Nelson initially took the *Victory* and the rest of his squadron on a fruitless hunt into the eastern Mediterranean before learning that they had in fact, sailed to the west. Nothing daunted, he followed the enemy, arriving in the West Indies in June, and hard on the heels of Villeneuve.

A starboard bow view of the most famous warship in the world, Admiral Horatio Nelson's immortal HMS *Victory*, still a serving unit in the Royal Navy, undergoing her latest in a long line of restorations at Portsmouth Naval Dockyard, October 2011. (World Copyright 2012 Peter C. Smith)

The French then sailed back across the Atlantic but their plan had not worked for the Channel Fleet still remained on station to thwart them, and with these vessels barring his way, and with Nelson again hard on his heels, the French Admiral took his ships into Cadiz where close watch was maintained on them by a British fleet under Admiral Collingwood.

The *Victory* returned to Spithead briefly but, by September, Nelson had rejoined Collingwood off Cadiz and on 19 October they received word that Villeneuve was coming out. The combined French

The imposing stern detail of the most famous warship in the world, Admiral Horatio Nelson's immortal HMS *Victory*, still a serving unit in the Royal Navy, undergoing her latest in a long line of restorations at Portsmouth Naval Dockyard, October 2011.
(World Copyright 2012 Peter C. Smith)

and Spanish fleets, totalling thirty-three ships, and the British fleet of twenty-seven ships, met off Cape Trafalgar on the 21st and the battle was finally joined once the British had got between the enemy and Cadiz, thus preventing flight.

The *Victory* led in to break the French line and at 1220 became engaged with Villeneuve's flagship *Buceutaure* and she received broadsides from seven enemy ships which caused some structural damage. Notwithstanding, *Victory* led on and was able to rake the stern of the *Buceutaure* with shot and grape, inflicting great carnage on her lower decks. She then closed with the *Redoutable*, while the *Temeraire* and the *Fougeux* also lay locked together in the same group exchanging broad-

sides. Nelson, quite conspicuous on *Victory's* deck during this close-range exchange, refused to take cover and at 1325 a sniper in the rigging of the *Redoutable* shot him through the left shoulder. He was taken below and died of his wounds some three hours later, but not before knowing that the battle was won. In all, the French and Spanish fleet lost nineteen of their ships and their ability to ensure the transport of the French Army to the English coast was shattered for good.

Victory herself suffered heavily in the engagement and was refitted at Chatham, before going out to the Baltic under Admiral Saumarez in 1808, while the following year she helped evacuate the Army from Corunna in Spain. She returned to the

A gun deck aboard the most famous warship in the world, Admiral Horatio Nelson's immortal HMS *Victory*, still a serving unit in the Royal Navy, undergoing her latest in a long line of restorations at Portsmouth Naval Dockyard, October 2011. (World Copyright 2012 Peter C. Smith)

The palatial and splendid Admiral's quarters aboard the most famous warship in the world, Admiral Horatio Nelson's immortal HMS *Victory*, still a serving unit in the Royal Navy, undergoing her latest in a long line of restorations at Portsmouth Naval Dockyard, October 2011. (World Copyright 2012 Peter C. Smith)

Baltic in 1809, blockading the Russian fleet, before again sailing to Portuguese waters flying the flag of Rear Admiral Yorke to support Wellington's land campaign. A further spell of duty in the Baltic followed, again under Saumarez, before she returned to her home port and was there paid off and decommissioned.

Between 1814 and 1816 the *Victory* was yet again extensively reconstructed but by the time she rejoined the fleet the war was finally over and she was laid up once again, this time as guard ship at Portsmouth. Here she remained until 1887 when she had to be docked for repairs due to leakage of her ancient hull. She stayed afloat off Gosport however, right through the First World War but had deteriorated considerably by 1920.

In 1922 the Society for Nautical Research, led by the Marquess of Milford Haven, initiated a scheme to help restore her to her condition at the time of Trafalgar. It was agreed that this should be done and in conjunction with the Admiralty, who continued to use her as the flagship of the Commander-in-Chief, Portsmouth, she entered No. 2 dry dock to become a permanent exhibition.

Further restoration followed the Second World War, when she suffered some bomb damage. In 1955 the Admiralty appointed the *Victory*

Advisory Technical Committee with representatives from the Society for Nautical Research and the Trustees of the National Maritime Museum, and they administered the *Victory*.

Thanks to their efforts, which still continue, the *Victory* can be seen today very much as Nelson knew her in 1805. A new contract for further essential reconstruction work on the *Victory* was issued in 2010 which will take future work through to 2019. The *Victory* currently retains her role as the flagship of the Commander-in-Chief Naval Home Command and combines this still by being a unique link between what little remains of the Royal Navy today and the great fleets of yesterday.

WARRIOR

When the *Warrior* was launched in 1860 she was the first fully armoured ship in the world. She rendered obsolete the 100-gun wooden 'three-deckers' which had remained almost unaltered from the old 'line-of-battle-ship' that had protected the nation ever since the days of Drake 300 years before. She was the forerunner of the *Dreadnought* and of the huge battleships of the twentieth century and as such she is unique.

Great Britain had remained unshakeable behind her bulwark of 'wooden walls and broadsides' and had built up an imposing strength of such mighty vessels and an incomparable expertise in their successful usage down those centuries. However, the long succession of defeats at sea suffered at the hands of the Royal Navy over the previous 200 years, had not dampened the ardour of the French for a long-awaited revenge,

HMS *Warrior*, the first modern battleship in the Royal Navy – a fine view from the top of the Spinnaker Tower with the almost empty naval dockyard beyond. (Copyright and Courtesy of Dawn & Sean Rayment)

and, in 1858, the new Directeur du Materiale of the French Navy had initiated the laying down of four revolutionary warships, all iron-clads, wooden-hulled warships with external iron plating attached to make them invulnerable to the heaviest guns. There was considerable alarm in Britain when this news leaked out in May of that year, and concerns were expressed that these vessels would wipe out Britain's long established superiority at sea.

It had always been the policy of the Royal Navy not to initiate new projects, confident that they

HMS *Warrior*, originally the first modern battleship in the Royal Navy and now one of the very best examples of detailed restorations of famous ships, makes an impressive study in power at Portsmouth Dockyard, October 2011. (World Copyright 2012 Peter C. Smith)

could always out-build and certainly out-fight their rivals should any threat arise, just as they had in the past, by the use of conventional vessels. Although earlier suggestions for building wooden ships 'sheathed in iron' had been turned down by the government, always then, as today, reluctant to spend money on defence, the knowledge of the French building programme caused some hasty re-thinking in Whitehall and the lights to be lit late into the night at the Admiralty.

In January 1859 therefore it was proposed to construct two iron-built frigates, *Warrior* and *Black Prince*, and the first, the *Warrior*, was entrusted to the builders with the overall specification that she should be able to overtake and destroy any other warship known to exist in the world. She was built at Blackwall on the Thames, being laid down in May 1859, launched in December 1860 and completed in August 1861. Thus, although the French *Couvonne* was laid down earlier, superior British shipbuilding enabled the *Warrior* to be the first sea-going iron warship to take to the water as a fighting vessel.

The actual armour built into the *Warrior* was of 11.43cm (4.5-inch) thickness laid on an 45.72cm (18-inch) teak backing and it embraced a central gun battery or citadel located amidships. Her guns originally were twenty-six 68-pounders and ten 110-pounders situated on her single gun deck and firing through gun ports. She was 115.824m

Looking along the port side of the magnificent broad sweep of the upper deck of HMS *Warrior*, the first modern battleship in the Royal Navy – (World Copyright 2012 Peter C. Smith)

(380ft) long between parallels with a breadth of 17.754m (58.25ft), and she had a tonnage of 9,210. Compare this with the *Victory*.

The early ironclads could not carry sufficient coal for prolonged passages on foreign stations and *Warrior* was therefore fitted with three masts carrying a total sail area of some 4,496.5m^2 (48,400ft^2). Under sail power alone she proved herself capable of 13 knots. Her machinery consisted of Penn's horizontal trunk single-expansion engines with indicated 5,000 h.p. and this made them the most powerful yet designed for a warship's propulsion. Boiler pressure was 9.071kg (20lbs) and during her trials the *Warrior* logged a speed of 14.3 knots. Her best performance utilising both sail and steam power was on 5 November 1861 when she made 16.3 knots. She had two telescopic funnels which could be lowered when proceeding under sail power alone.

Detail, showing the funnel and ventilators of the three-masted HMS *Warrior*, the first modern battleship in the Royal Navy in their mid-Victorian paint scheme. (World Copyright 2012 Peter C. Smith)

Her armament was modified before her completion and she carried eight of the new Armstrong Screw Breech 110-pounders on her main deck, four each side, together with twenty-six 68-pounders, while on her upper deck two 110-pounders and four 70-pounders were mounted, the latter for use as saluting guns.

Although rated as a frigate, the *Warrior*, when she first appeared, was far more powerful than the largest of the old first-rate battleships then in commission, which presented the Admiralty with a problem of classification. Hitherto it had been simple, for warships were classified as first-rate, second-rate, third-rate, etc, simply on the numbers of heavy guns they carried. By way of compromise the Admiralty decided to rate the *Warrior* according to the number of officers and men she carried and, accordingly, she was listed as a third-rate, although quite capable of easily destroying any first-rate she met in battle. The increasing numbers of such vessels built naturally soon rendered this old rating system unworkable and new classifications were later introduced which eventually crystallised in the early twentieth century as the battleship, cruiser, destroyer, minesweeper and so on, according to function.

However rated, when the *Warrior* first appeared and joined the fleet she caused quite a stir both at home and abroad. The French Emperor knew the game was up once more, calling the two British ironclads 'black snakes among the sheep' and knew his designs on wresting Britain's maritime crown had once more been nullified. As Admiral Ballard was later to record, there would now certainly be no French Army drum-majors swinging their batons down the Old Kent Road after all! For the next forty years there followed a succession of varied and often conflicting designs for the warships of the fleet as the pace of technological progress quickened throughout the second half of the nineteenth century. It was not until the 1890s that battleship development came to a stability of design and construction, which was not again upset until the arrival of the all big-gun battleship *Dreadnought* in 1906.

The *Warrior* was commissioned at Portsmouth in October 1861 and she served with the Channel Fleet for the next three years, her duties including acting as escort to the Royal Yacht bringing Princess Alexandra from Denmark. She then underwent a long refit between 1864 and 1867 when she was re-armed with four 20.3cm (8-inch) and twenty-eight 17.78cm (7-inch) muzzle-loading guns. This completed, she again joined the Channel Fleet until 1872 when a further refit involved the fitting of a poop and a steam capstan. By this time she had been surpassed in the fleet but she was still held in high esteem in the Navy and great affection. A further period of service followed with the duties of Guard ship at Portland until, in 1881, she became the training ship on the Clyde for the Royal Naval Reserve. This was her last period of duty but when she paid off in 1884 she was still retained on the Navy List as an 'armoured cruiser', although by this date her fighting value was nil.

In 1904 the *Warrior* found fresh employment as a torpedo depot ship at Portsmouth and was attached to the *Vernon* torpedo and mine establishment until the completion of the shore facilities.

She was then cut down and reduced to the lowly status of oil pipeline pier at Pembroke Dock. For many subsequent decades she lay, dirty, forgotten and isolated at Milford Haven as an oiling berth. The National Maritime Museum and The Maritime Trust finally took joint action to persuade the Ministry of Defence to release her to them for preservation; meanwhile, the few remaining artefacts were removed in advance for safe keeping. Her huge figurehead, which was among the very last to be fitted to the prows of a British battleship, was one of these which was rescued from decay and rot and preserved at Portsmouth until the rest of the ship was ready.

Unique as the forerunner of the battleship of the twentieth century the *Warrior* is as historically important as the *Victory* and the *Cutty Sark* to our maritime history and naval heritage. The restoration of HMS *Warrior* has been skilfully and lovingly carried out and she now presents a magnificent picture of British seapower at its peak.

M-33

The monitor as a class of warship with shallow draught that enabled them to operate in coastal waters and a range of medium to heavy guns with which to bombard targets ashore has now vanished from the Royal Navy, along with battleships, battle-cruisers, cruisers, minelayers and others that were once basic naval types. This type of vessel took its generic name from an American vessel of the Civil War era which had these characteristics, although not designed as such. A large number of monitors served during the First World War and their guns ranged from the very largest (a 45.72cm (18-inch) monster originally designed for the battle-cruiser *Furious* which bombarded the German army along the Belgian coast and also lock gates and docks to block them to U-boats later in the war, down to small weapons employed up the rivers of Mesopotamia and Africa.

The *M-29* class monitors comprised a group of five ships, *M-29*, *M-30*, *M-31*, *M-32* and *M-33*, that came into being when it was decided that the new Queen Elizabeth-class battleships then building each had two spare Mark XII 15.2cm (6-inch) guns which were not required and were to be landed ashore. It was thought these ten weapons could be gainfully employed as coastal bombardment weapons for Admiral Jackie Fisher's bold, if somewhat impractical, idea of despatching a fleet of such warships to the Baltic and landing an army close to Berlin. That idea never took place, but another operation, to force the Dardanelles and by anchoring a fleet off Constantinople, force Turkey out of the war, did. A design was quickly sketched out by Assistant Naval Constructor Charles S. Lillicrap and these five little vessels were quickly built in Belfast shipyards, three by Harland & Wolff and two, *M-32* and *M-33*, by Workman Clark. In fact the guns that were

actually fitted turned out to be two of the brand new 15.2cm (6-inch) 45-calibre BL Mk XII mountings built at Coventry Ordnance Works with barrels from the Vickers company, mounted one forward and one aft.

Building of all these little ships was incredibly swift; they were all approved on 15 March 1915, and *M-33* herself was laid down on 1 April, launched on 22 May with completion on 17 June 1915 and commissioned for service under the command of Lieutenant Commander Q. B. Preston-Thomas on 24 June. Nowadays it takes five or six years to plan a warship and about the same time to build it, but back then they got the job done and, as *M-33* was to demonstrate, they also built to last! Their particulars were a displacement of 355 tons, a full load displacement of 580 tons, an overall length of 54.03m (177ft 3in), a beam of 9.4m (31ft) and a 1.8m (5.11in) draught. She was powered by 400ihp (indicated horse power) (300kW) @ 250 rpm 2-shaft VTE, triple-expansion engine, which gave a best speed of 9.5 knots and carried 45 tons of fuel oil. She had a range of 2,670km (1,440 nautical miles) at a speed of 8 knots. She had no defensive armour other than the 15.2cm (6-inch) plating on the front of each of her gun shields. This monitor was also armed with a single 57mm (6pdr) quick-firing Hotchkiss anti-aircraft gun and two .303-inch Maxim machine guns. She had a complement of five officers and sixty-seven men.

The original plan conceived by Winston Churchill and Lord Fisher to force the Dardenelles in a daring stroke had failed due to a combination of a string of German supplied mines protected by heavy guns ashore, and British command inertia. Thus the fatal decision was taken to land an army, destroy the forts, allow the mines to be swept and then proceed. Alas it all came to nothing but the resultant Gallipoli Peninsula campaign mirrored the carnage of the Western Front.

The *M-33* arrived at the Dardanelles on 24 July 1915 and provided covering fire for further troop landings on 2 August. Her next action was on 6/7 August when *M-33* was part of a force that gave counter-battery fire in the Cape Helles–Anzac Cover sector, when she was hit by shell splinters from a near miss which peppered her upperworks. This hot work was maintained even though the recoil of her main guns caused some internal damage to her lightly-built bulkheads

The First World War monitor *M-33*, the last example of a specialist shallow-draught warship with heavy guns designed for littoral warfare. She fought against the Turks in the Mediterranean and in 1919 against the Bolsheviks in North Russia.
(World Copyright 2012 Peter C. Smith)

and inner beams. She continued firing until 14 August, when she was relieved by the monitor *Humber* and underwent a refit where this damage was repaired and her decks reinforced. This work completed, *M-33* resumed operations off the beachheads through to December. But it had become abundantly clear that the campaign had been a costly failure and plans were in hand to evacuate the British and ANZAC forces totally, which was successfully achieved.

The *M-33* remained in the Mediterranean and on 11 January 1916 was part of the Allied Fleet that assisted in the setting up of an Allied base at Stavros, on the north-western coast of Greece, which was to act as a supply port for the Salonika campaign in Bulgaria. On 29 March the *M-33* suffered one of the first air attacks made on warships when three Bulgarian aircraft attacked her but she was not hit. Nor was her return AA fire very effective. The *M-33* was the guard ship of this important anchorage for a period.

During a bombardment mission off Cape Aspro, in the Gulf of Smyrna (Izmir) on the night of 13/14 May 1916, return Turkish howitzer fire hit her sister ship the *M-30* in her engine room. One shell disabled her Yarrow engines and started a large fire. There were many casualties but about fifty of the crew, including many wounded, were rescued from the blazing ship by the armed motor yacht *California* and the monitor sank shortly afterwards. The *M-30* was beached and abandoned on Uzunada (Long Island), but the *M-33* went in under heavy shell fire and assisted in salvaging her guns so that they would not fall into enemy hands. Then she provided covering fire while the wireless telegraph station and the airstrip on the island were evacuated. Along with the sloop *Peterborough* the *M-33* continued blockading the Gulf and carrying out frequent bombardments. She had fifty heavy shells aimed at her but none hit, and in response she silenced two Turkish gun batteries. Covering a raiding force of Greek irregulars on the Turkish mainland *M-33* was attacked from the air for a second time, again without damage, but her companion, the gunboat *Oomala* was hit and *M-33* had to tow her out of the area.

On 17 May she sailed for Kephalo and became part of a squadron attempting to knock out a Turkish long-range gun which was causing considerable irritation in the area. This gun engaged the ships, one heavy shell dropping some 9.144m (ten yards) from the *M-33*. *M-33*'s return fire was reported by spotting aircraft to have destroyed an Ottoman ammunition dump. The monitors of this squadron, *Raglan*, *M-19*, *M-28*, *M-29*, *M-32* and *M-33* then sailed to Stavros where they fired on Bulgarian troops at Kavala, knocking down the post office, custom house and military barrack block. The *M-33* herself conducted bombardments of Turkish positions during a raid on the Turkish mainland in July and along with her sister *M-32*, was sent to join a French naval force carrying out bombardments on the southern Turkish coast in August and on 1 September was present at Salamis when the Greek fleet was quarantined. She continued operations off the Aegean coast of Turkey through to the end of the year, before sailing for Mudros, where she went into the floating dock for an overhaul.

Christmas found her back in action as part of the covering force for another Greek operation and between February and April 1917 was based at Syra in the Aegean once more, before returning to Mudros. She was based at Stavros, then another refit at Mudros before sailing for Mitylene to help establish the base there. She again refitted at Mudros between January and February 1918 and continued Aegean operations to July, when her new captain, Commander H. Haire-Foster, took command. Along with the monitors *Abercrombie* and *M-32*, the *M-33* was again in action against the Turks at Stavros firing fifty rounds of 15.2cm (6-inch) shell into Ottoman lines. She suffered no damage in reply but was accidently rammed by a K-lighter and had to be detached to Salonika for repair. Here her third CO, Commander L. W. Patch, took command. With the cessation of hostilities and thirty-nine months of continuous commission, the crew of the *M-33* were to be sent home on leave while a new crew took over. *M-33*'s last official duty in the First World War was to oversee the armistice with the Turks, after which she left for Mudros, finally paying off on 19 January 1919.

The forward 15.2cm (6-inch gun) mounting aboard the First World War monitor *M33*, the last example of a specialist shallow-draught warship with heavy guns designed for littoral warfare. (World Copyright 2012 Peter C. Smith)

The new captain and crew re-commissioned *M-33* on 26 February 1919 and she sailed for the United Kingdom, arriving at Chatham on 10 April where she underwent a complete overhaul in readiness for her next wartime duties. Both the *M-32* and *M-33* had their 6-pounder guns replaced by a more efficient 7.62cm (3-inch)/20cwt AA weapon and four Lewis guns and two extra Maxims were embarked. Both ships then sailed from Sheerness for the Shetland Islands and at Lerwick the trawler *Carbill* took over and towed her as far as Tromsö, Norway where she was forced to idle until the ice sheets cleared enough for her to continue on to Archangel, where she finally arrived on 9 June.

Here they were assigned as part of the Royal Navy expeditionary force sent to aid the White Russian forces who were attempting to overthrow the Bolsheviks during the Civil War that was raging. Along with the *M-24*, *M-25*, *M-26*, *M-27* and *M-31* she acted as Relief Force. The *M-33* operated in that theatre between May and September 1919, being based at Murmansk for the Dvina River campaign under the command of Lieutenant Commander Kenneth Mitchell. Her crew at this time were listed as being a Surgeon Lieutenant, a Navigating Officer, a Commissioned Gunner, thirty-eight seamen, fifteen engine-room ratings, ten Royal Marines and seven cooks, stewards and medical ratings.

To lend fire support to the White Army the *M-33* navigated the river Dvina up to Bereznik and it was here, on 16 June, that she was subjected to air attack for the third time, by three Red Army aircraft, again without damage to either side. The *M-33* carried out bombardments directed by a spotter seaplane and kite balloons firing off some 200 rounds of 15.2cm (6-inch) shell at Seltso and Selemengo Wood. Their efforts were rather nullified, however, when the White Russian troops mutinied on 7 July, but *M-33* continued in action that day and on the 8th received a shell hit from the Bolshevik artillery that ended up in the ship's wardroom; fortunately there were no casualties. A month later she was again hit twice, and her steering gear was damaged, while a second shell went through the Petty Officers' Mess into the engine room, but failed to detonate. In response *M-33* fired off another 150 shells at the enemy.

It was decided to withdraw all British forces and while covering the evacuations on 18 August she narrowly escaped being mined. The river downstream had silted up since their original advance and in order to safely navigate the shallows they had to raise her draught by a full foot and to achieve this some ten tons of equipment, including guns, shells, the mast, internal fittings and much fuel had to be unceremoniously ditched. To give the appearance she was fully operational dummy guns were manufactured from biscuit tins, old pipes and wooden crates. She reached Archangel on 29 August while her guns duly followed some weeks later on barges. The *M-25* and *M-27* were not so lucky; being bigger and of greater draught they ran aground while making the same journey and had to be blown up on 16 September. Once her guns were re-fitted *M-33* went some way back upriver to provide covering fire at Spaskoe for the final 500 withdrawing British soldiers. All British forces had pulled out of North Russia by 27 September and later sailed for home.

The *M-33* reached Chatham on 17 October where she was paid off and used as a tender for a while until being laid up at the Nore. The *M-33* was then converted into a coastal minelaying training vessel at Pembroke Dock between May 1924 and February 1925. This involved taking out her main armament and the fitting of mine rails which could accommodate both fifty-two H-type moored mines and ground mines. She was attached to the Royal Navy Mining Establishment, HMS *Vernon*, at Portsmouth and renamed as *Minerva* in December, becoming the fifteenth ship to bear that name in the Royal Navy.

In 1930 she was again laid up and this brief period of 'active' service ended. In 1937 she was placed on the sales list, but, on outbreak of war, she was reprieved and in September 1939 she was renamed as Hulk *C-23* and used as floating offices for the WRNS. She was scheduled to become a refuelling hulk at Gosport, but, instead, turned up at Southampton in November 1943 where useful wartime employ was found for her as a Boom Defence Workshop. Later, she was towed up to the Clyde in December 1944 where she acted as part of the boom defence system. In 1946, with the war over, she was returned to Portsmouth once more to resume duties as a floating office and workshop. She was assigned to the Fleet Auxiliary vessels based at Royal Clarence Victualling Yard at Gosport, where she languished as the RMAS *Minerva* Hulk *C-23*. Finally, in 1984, she was yet again put up for sale.

Some people still remembered her origins, however, and sought to rescue her. In 1987 the Hartlepool Ship Preservation Trust bought her. She was hoisted on a barge and taken to the north-east where the plan was to fully restore her at Hartlepool. But, in the end, funds proved insufficient and only her funnel was restored. Another rescuer appeared, and in 1990 Hampshire County Council purchased her and the following year she was towed back to Portsmouth Naval dockyard. Here an arrangement was made whereby the Royal Naval Museum managed the *M-33* on behalf of Hampshire County Council Museums Service. Painting of the ship's upperworks took place, the forward 15.2cm (6-inch) gun was installed aboard and she reverted to her original designation as *M-33*.

Hampshire County Council took over the restoration work in 1995, again with the intent of restoring her to her Great War state. New masts were installed, a Mark XII 15.2cm (6-inch) gun unearthed from HMS *Excellent* was fitted on her fo'c'sle and, in 1997 she was dry-docked in No. 1 Basin where the extensive rust damage was tackled. The following year her old hull was made fully watertight. Modern technology came to her aid in 2000 when a new electrolytic technique was used on her, which removed chlorides from between her riveted joints. Between that date and 2006 work continued apace both internally and externally. New artefacts like anchors, gun-shields and the like were cloned, while a genuine 15.2cm (6-inch) gun was located by the Chilean Navy. It was a relic from the battleship *Almirante Latorre* which had been building in England at Armstrong's shipyard on the outbreak of war in 1914, and which had been purchased by the Admiralty and renamed *Canada.* She had served with the Grand Fleet and had been present at the Battle of Jutland. She had reverted to Chile in April 1920 and it was the Chilean Navy who presented the gun to *M-33* where it was duly emplaced aft. In 2007 the *M-33* was painted in the dazzle camouflage pattern that she had carried in 1918, to present a striking contrast to the adjacent HMS *Victory.*

HOLLAND-1

The very first submarine to serve in the Royal Navy and of enormous historic importance now that her giant successors are the most powerful warships ever built and provide Great Britain's nuclear deterrent shield against aggressor states. Although the submarine had found favour aboard, many senior officers of the Royal Navy shared the view that it was 'a damned un-English' weapon and many dismissed it as an unnecessary, and, worse, an underhanded weapon of war. Others were more visionary, Admiral Jackie Fisher among them, and foresaw an incredible future for them, but even he would have been amazed (although probably approved) of the monsters of

The port bow view of the Royal Navy's very first submarine, the *Holland-1*, as a walk-through exhibit at the Gosport Submarine Museum at Gosport. (World Copyright 2012 Peter C. Smith)

Stern view of the Royal Navy's very first submarine, the *Holland-1*, now on show as a walk-through museum exhibit at the Gosport Submarine Museum at Gosport. (World Copyright 2012 Peter C. Smith)

the deep of the twenty-first century which are the true battleships of today's fleet. From the 1870s onward inventors like the Italian Cesare Laurenti and the American Simon Lake were arousing interest while the designs of an Irish émigré to the United States, John Philip Holland, proved among the first practical designs of the late nineteenth century. As foreign navies like France and the United States appeared eager to develop this, as yet, novel and untried naval weapon, the Admiralty decided to see what the potential really was, even though the then First Lord considered there was no need for them. They entered negotiations with Mr John Philip Holland's Electric Boat Company at Groton, Connecticut, which had

been founded in 1899 to build Holland's submersibles, and the result was an outline agreement to construct, under licence, five boats of the latest design in Great Britain. Treasury funding was sought, and obtained.

The *No. 1*, as she was known in service, was officially ordered in December 1900 and laid down on 4 February 1901 at Vickers shipyard at Barrow in Furness, Cumbria, being launched on 2 October the same year but not completed until 2 February 1903. She had an overall length of 19.20m (63ft 10in) and a beam of 3.35m (11ft 10in). Her displacement was 113 tons when surfaced and 122 tons submerged and she had a diving depth of 100 feet. She had a single shaft with three-bladed, 1.82m (6ft) diameter propeller and a designed surface speed of 8 knots, but only attained 7.4 knots in service, while her submerged speed was 7 knots as designed and 6 knots in actual operations. She had a designed surface range of 571.317km (355 miles) but only 378.195km (235 miles) actual and a submerged reach of 32.186km (20 miles) at an economical 5 knots speed.

She recorded the first-ever dive by a Royal Navy submarine on 5 February 1902 during her sea trials, which lasted until April. Being used

The torpedo-launching tubes in the bows of the Royal Navy's very first submarine, the *Holland-1*, now a walk-through museum exhibit at the Gosport Submarine Museum at Gosport. (World Copyright 2012 Peter C. Smith)

almost exclusively at first as a trials' ship, she was beaten into service by *No. 2* but, although considered very primitive, these five boats gave the Navy sufficient food for thought that the sixth vessel, was modified considerably and served as the prototype for the all-British A-class submarines and the rapid development of the type has been continuous ever since. *No.1* continued to be employed exclusively as an experimental and training vessel, being based at Fort Blockhouse, Portsmouth until 1913 when she was sold for scrap.

The *No. 1* was sold for scrap in October 1913, but foundered off the Eddystone Lighthouse, Plymouth Sound, while under tow from Portsmouth to the breakers' yard and was lost for almost seventy years. She was discovered on the seabed in April 1981. Later that summer the diving support vessel *Seaforth Clansman* was positioned over the wreck and commenced carefully clearing seventy years of accumulated debris away for her to be lifted up and deposited in shallower water off Drake's Island preparatory to the next stage. The *Holland-1*'s batteries were then removed to lighten her further. The Royal Marine Auxiliary Service Vessel *Pintail* again raised the *Holland-1* in November 1982 and she was taken into Devonport Dockyard where she was carefully lowered onto a specially-prepared cradle in No. 12 dock. When the dock had been pumped out, careful cleaning using water blasting was carried out externally and internally; DMP Marine treated both surfaces with Fertan, a chemical compound which 'de-rusted' the old metal. The Dockyard then cut her into three pieces so that she could be transported by road by the Royal Corps of Transport to Gosport.

She is now a walk-through Museum exhibit at the Gosport Submarine Museum where I was able to photograph her.

X-CRAFT – X-7, X-24, XE-8 AND STICKLEBACK (X-51)

Commonly known as Midget Submarines, these X-craft owed their immediate origins to a very small submarine designed to be used by the Army in rivers like the Rhine and Elbe. The prototypes were laid down in 1939. They were the brainchild of Commander Cromwell H. Varley DSC RN who later designed the X-3 which underwent trials off Scotland in October 1942. (The X-1 had been a large submarine built in 1925 and X-2 had been allocated to a captured Italian submarine.) Commander T. I. S. Bell DSC RN was another officer who was later in charge of personnel and training for the X-craft. A Royal Naval shore base, formerly the Kyles of Bute Hydropathic Hotel, was named after them, HMS *Varbel* at Kames Bay, Isle of Bute and the Ardtaraig House shooting lodge on Loch Striven was taken over as *Varbel II* with the drifter *Present Help* as their tender.

The two early prototypes X-3 and X-4 were built by Varley Marine with help from Portsmouth Dockyard. The Flag Officer Submarines, Admiral Sir Max Horton, was an enthusiastic backer of the idea. His successor, Admiral Berry, thought that more time was required to train the crews on these missions and postponed operations until the end of the Arctic summer. Twenty were built in several different groups, the general particulars being a surface displacement of 27 tons, a submerged displacement of 30 tons, with an overall length of 15.62m (51.25ft), a beam of 1.75m (5.75ft) and a 1.6m (5.3ft) draught. They had a single Gardner 4-cylinder diesel engine (an adaptation of those that drove the famous London Transport buses) developing 31.3kW (42hp) at 1,800 rpm and a Keith Blackman 22.3kW (30hp) electric motor which gave a surfaced speed of 6.5 knots (12km/h) and submerged speed of 5.5 knots (10.1km/h).

They had an estimated range of 804.672km (500 miles) on the surface and 131.966km (82 miles) submerged at 2 knots and were test dived to around 91.5m (300ft). They had a crew of four, including a diver who could leave the vessel to attach limpet mines when required.

Each X-craft had two detachable 'side cargoes' which were to be released beneath the target vessel, each one containing two tons of Amatex high explosive. Each was fitted with clockwork time fuses. The Midgets had to be towed to the attack zone by conventional submarines, either S- or T-class boats, with a towing crew aboard, while the four-man attack crew replaced them prior to the mission. This team included a diver who could also individually attach up to six 20lb limpet mines to a suitable mercantile target. Eventually three wartime types were produced, the X-craft, used in European waters; the larger XE-craft, designed for the Far East with more habitable conditions and the XT-craft, designed for training of crews.

The first midgets were launched in March 1942, X-5 to X-10 and became operational in 1943. Captain John F. Beaufoy Brown, former captain of the famous submarine *Taku* and Max Horton's Staff Officer, commanded *Varbel II* as Midget Submarine Base and Training Officer from 1943 to 1945. Under his tenure the famous attack that crippled the German battleship *Tirpitz* in Altenfiord, Norway, Operation SOURCE, took place in September 1943. Six X-craft were despatched but only two survived to lay their charges, but the resulting explosions badly damaged the *Tirpitz*, which remained out of action for seven months.

Further operations by X-craft in Norway followed this success. On 14 April 1944 the 7,500-ton

German merchant ship *Barenfels* was sunk in Operation GUIDANCE by the *X-24* under the command of the Australian Lieutenant Commander Max H. Shean, RANVR, towed into the area by the submarine *Sceptre*. The *X-24* also took part in Operation HECKLE, an attack on the large floating dock at Laksvaag, Bergen, Norway on 11 September. Making her way for 48.28km (30 miles) up the heavily protected and patrolled fiord to Bergen in broad daylight, her commanding officer, now Lieutenant H. P. Westmacott DSC RN, who had earlier commanded the submarine

X-24 on display at Gosport in the John Fieldhouse Building at the Royal Navy Submarine Museum.
(Copyright 2012 Peter C. Smith)

Unshaken, made her attack early that morning. The target was a German-built dock towed up to Norway to service the *Tirpitz* and also used for U-boat repairs. It was split in half by the resulting explosions along with two ships, the *Sten* and the *Kong Oscar II*. The *X-24* was safely back in the Shetlands by 13 September. On both these occasions the *X-24* was towed into and out of the zone by the submarine *Sceptre* (Lieutenant Ian McIntosh RN).

X-craft were also involved in the Normandy landings in June 1944, the *X-20* making reconnaissance missions over a four day period beforehand in Operation POSTAGE ABLE. Later she was joined by the *X-23* who, at 0445 on the morning of 6 June 1944, surfaced off the beaches and erected their 5.48m (18ft) tall navigation beacons and activated them. These incorporated a seaward-only green position light and had radio beacon and echo sounding equipment that guided in the minesweepers towards the British beachheads. The Americans refused the offer of such guides and their convoys went somewhat astray.

Of the six late-built boats built by Markham's of Chesterfield, the *X-20*, *X-21*, *X-22*, *X-23*, *X-24* and *X-25*, one, *X-22*, was sunk with all hands on 7 February 1944 after a collision with the submarine *Syrtis* in the Pentland Firth. There were gale-force winds and high seas in the Firth at the time, and the officer of the watch aboard the *Syrtis* was washed over the side. The submarine turned to try and rescue him but, in so doing, immediately ran down the *X-22* which she was towing. Four of the five surviving X-boats were all scrapped when the war was over, but the *X-24*, having being retired in 1950, was mounted on the sea wall at HMS *Dolphin* but, after ten years there exposed to the elements, was moved inside the base. Another decade passed and then two surveys were made of her, in October 1970 and January 1971. In January 1972 the long-delayed decision was made to preserve her as a memorial and she was taken by road to Portsmouth Dockyard, fully restored and returned for display.

The Vickers-built *XT-1*, *XT-2*, *XT-3*, *XT-4*, *XT-5* and *XT-6* were completed between 1943 and 1945 as training boats, and were a simplified design

based on the *X-5* but with a fixed day periscope only and without the release gear for the side-packs or an automatic helmsman being fitted. All were scrapped post-war and a further twelve XT boats, which were ordered from Broadbent, Huddersfield, were cancelled while still building.

Later Beaufoy Brown took the 14th Submarine Flotilla out to the Far East, for which work he received the OBE. This flotilla comprised the larger XE-craft *XE-1*, *XE-2*, *XE-3*, *XE-4*, *XE-5* and *XE-6*, which were of 30.25 tons surfaced displacement, 33.5 tons submerged, and 16.23m (53.25ft) overall length, with a 1.75m (5.75ft) beam and a draught of 1.6m (5ft 3in). They were all built by Thomas Broadbent and Sons, had a single Gardner 4-cycle diesel engine of 42hp (31.3kW) at 1,800rpm which gave them a surface speed of 6.5 knots and a submerged speed of 5.5 knots, while their range was 926km (500 nautical miles) on the surface and 152km (82 nautical miles) submerged. They were tested to a depth of 90m (300ft) and had a crew of five.

By the time they arrived in the Far East at the island of Labuan off the northern coast of Borneo with the depot ship *Bonaventure*, the Pacific War was virtually over. Nonetheless, having come that far, the crews were determined to use them in action. Suitable targets were still to be found. The powerful Japanese heavy cruisers *Myôkô* and *Takao*[2] (each of 13,400 tons, ten 20.3cm (8-inch) guns), for example, were known to be anchored at the Singapore naval base and it was decided to attack them with the *XE-1* and *XE-3* via the Johore Strait in Operation STRUGGLE. The two X-craft were under the guidance of the submarine *Stygian* and, on 31 July 1945, they penetrated all the Japanese defences. The *XE-3* managed to close with her target, the *Takao*, releasing both of her side charges and also affixed limpet mines to the cruiser and made a successful withdrawal, all without detection or reaction. Her companion, the *XE-1*, could not locate the *Myôkô* and so added her charges to those beneath *Takao*, and

---

2. *Takao* had been damaged so badly at the Battle of Leyte Gulf in October 1944 that she was not seaworthy and was being used for defensive purposes with only a skeleton crew.

also made a clean escape. When the charges detonated, the *Takao*, already damaged by two submarine torpedoes at the Battle of Leyte Gulf, was further damaged and settled on the harbour bottom. These were tough ships and post-war she was raised from the seabed, taken out to sea and scuttled in the Malacca Straits on 27 October 1946, where the *Myôkô* had already been scuttled on 8 July. The crews duly received true recognition for their bravery: Lieutenant Ian Fraser, RNR and Leading Seaman James J. Magennis were awarded the Victoria Cross, while all the other crew members received awards ranging from the DSO, DSC and CGM to the MID.

Two further operations were conducted by the XE-craft under the leadership of Captain W. R. Fell CBE DSC RN designed to cut the underwater telephone cables linking Tokyo with Singapore and Hong Kong. The *XE-4*, towed by the submarine *Spearhead*, conducted Operation SABRE, and cut the two cables linking Saigon in Vichy-French-owned, Japanese-occupied French Indo-China, and Singapore, while the *XE-5*, towed by the submarine *Selene*, carried out Operation FOIL and severed the cable off Lamma Island southwest of Hong Kong cutting the link from Hong Kong to Saigon. She became entangled for ninety-six hours but her two divers, Sub Lieutenant D. V. M. Jarvis DSC RNVR and Lieutenant B. G. Clarke DSC RNVR, finally managed to cut her free. Despite these successes all six of these craft were scrapped in 1945.

Four further XE-boats were built, *XE-7* and *XE-8* by Thomas Broadbent and *XE-9* and *XE-10* by Markham, while two of an improved type, *XE-11* and *XE-12*, were built by Marshall. The end of the war saw no perceived use for them and they were soon disposed of. The *XE-11* had been lost in an accident during training in Loch Striven on 6 March 1945 with the death of three of her five-man crew. She was later salvaged and scrapped. The *XE-6* was scrapped in 1952 while *XE-12* was also broken up in 1952 and *XE8*, which her crew under Canadian Johnnie C. Rise had named *Expunger* with the motto 'The fewer the men, the greater the honour', was sunk as a target the same year. Not until 1973 was she recovered from the seabed and preserved as an exhibit at Chatham Historical Dockyard, where she is still only able to be viewed externally. The *XE-9* was lent with her British crew to the US Navy in October 1952 to aid their work on a midget submarine programme of their own before being scrapped.

Post-war a further development was the building of four Stickleback-class boats, improved versions of the XE types, classified as Midget XPW, which were built by Vickers Armstrong. These submarines were the *Stickleback (X-51)* launched on 1 October 1954, *Shrimp (X-52)* launched 30 December 1954, *Sprat (X-53)* launched 1 March 1955 and *Minnow (X-54)* launched 5 May 1955. They were designed originally purely as training vehicles for British defences as the Soviet Union was thought to have developed such vessels. They had a displacement of 35.2 tons on the surface and 39.27 tons submerged, and had an overall length of 15.44m (50ft 8in) between parallels, and 16.41m (53ft 10in) overall, with a beam of 1.8m (6ft) and a draught of 2.29m (7ft 6in). Their propulsion was by a Perkins P6 6-cycle diesel and a 50bhp/44shp electric motor which gave them a surface speed of 6.5 knots and a submerged speed of 6 knots. They had a crew of five.

The *Stickleback* was sold to the Royal Swedish Navy on 15 July 1958 and became their *Spiggen*, while the *Sprat*, with a British crew commanded by Lieutenant T. J. Anderson RN, was transferred to the US Navy in 1958 for three months of trials in developing their own midget submarines, being transported aboard the USS *Alcor* on 19 June 1958 and arriving at Norfolk, Virginia on 2 July. She was returned to the UK on 3 September aboard the USS *Antares*. Eventually the *Shrimp* was broken up at Rosyth in 1965; the *Minnow* and *Sprat* were both scrapped at Faslane in 1966. The *Stickleback* was returned in 1977 and became a museum ship.

In 1955–56 a more offensive role was envisaged for such craft had the Cold War gone hot and that was the depositing of 15-kiloton nuclear mines in the top secret strategic Soviet harbours of Kronstadt, Murmansk and Archangel. Based on the Red Beard tactical nuclear bomb then being deployed on Royal Navy aircraft, this weapon would have taken out whole port areas at a stroke and was codenamed Operation CUDGEL. The Director of Undersurface Warfare, Captain P. J. Cowell, requested funding for a new type of 30-ton, two-man X-craft constructed of non-magnetic metal, whose *raison d'etre* was to be towed in by a Porpoise-class submarine to within 241.401km (150 miles) of the target and then for the X-craft to effect the undetected delivery of an atomic bomb and return the crew to the parent submarine. The device was timed so that it would activate a week later. As with so many other British defence concepts, a good idea was aborted due to lack of funding to develop the atomic mine and no further X-craft were built.

Three midget submarines have been preserved – the *XE-8* (*Expunger*) is on display at Chatham Historic Dockyard which I visited in October 2011 and since 2005 the *X-24* has been displayed in the John Fieldhouse Building at the Royal Navy Submarine Museum, Haslar Jetty Road, Gosport, Hants PO12 2AS, which I also viewed the same month. The *Stickleback* (*X-51*) is currently on sectioned display at the Imperial War Museum site at Duxford, Cambridge and the remnants of the *X-7* are also held here. As a footnote, the strange-looking Midget on outside display at Chatham Historic Dockyard between the *Gannet* and *Ocelot*, has no significant maritime historical import, other than to film buffs, it having been built specifically for one of the James Bond 007 film epics!

ALLIANCE

The last Second World War design submarines built for the Royal Navy were the A-class boats, designed under the War Emergency Programme for operations in the Pacific Ocean against the Japanese Navy. For this they needed far greater range and better habitability than the average submarine then in service and operating in European and Mediterranean waters. With this in mind, a large new class of submarine was designed and laid down in the years 1943–45 but not finally completed until the war was over, in 1945–48. Sixteen were finally built, thirty were cancelled and a further order for another twenty was also scrapped before any work was done. The *Alliance* (P417 and later S67) was one of those which survived the cull, being laid down on 13 March 1945, launched on 28 July 1945 from Vickers Armstrong yard at Barrow-in-Furness but not finally commissioned for service until 14 May 1947.

Previous Royal Navy ships named *Alliance* included a sixth-rate Dutch vessel named *Alliante*, (20-guns) which was made a prize off the Norwegian coast on 22 August in 1795 and renamed. She served at the battle of Acre in 1799, later being made over into a store-ship and was finally sold out in May 1802. There was also an Admiralty tug which had been launched on 23 August 1910 and which survived until 19 December 1941, when, during the Japanese capture of Hong Kong, she was scuttled in Deepwater Bay. The submarine *Alliance* became the third ship to carry the name.

The A-class submarines were built with the circular section welded pressure hull with 1.905cm (0.75-inch) plating which was designed to operate to depths of 152.4m (500ft) and were tested to 182.88m (600ft) as an emergency maximum depth. They were the first British submarines to be designed from scratch to carry the Snorkel device which allowed air to be drawn in while the boat was still submerged. Although not all were so fitted on completion due to peacetime cutbacks, the *Alliance* had one from the start. They had a standard displacement of 1,120 tons, and 1,590 tons submerged. Their dimensions were 85.11m (279ft 3in) overall with a 6.78 m (22ft 3in) beam and a 5.21m (17ft 1in) maximum draught at normal loading. Their power plant was 2-shaft Vickers 8-cylinder, single-acting, four-stroke super-charged diesel engines each developing 2,150bhp at 460rpm plus two sets of Direct-Drive electric motors each developing 625bhp and driving twin three-bladed screws of 1.524m (5ft 9in) diameter, which gave them a surfaced speed of 18.5 knots and a submerged maximum speed of 8 knots. They carried 165 tons of oil fuel (60 tons internal tanks, 105 tons in external tanks) 219 tons maximum with 54 tons in the main tanks. They were credited with a range of 19,400km (10,500 nautical miles). They were armed with ten 53.34cm (21-inch) torpedo-tubes, whose torpedoes weighed 1,112.308kg (3,452lbs), with four tubes in the bow, two in the stern and four external, two in the bows and two astern. The Mk 8** torpedo was a very old design but considered reliable as a simple 'aim and fire' submarine weapon. The running depth could be manually set while in the tube before firing, as could a gyro angle controlled course, commencing about 36.576m (40 yards) from leaving the tube, with three choices of pre-setting; 90 degrees left or zero or 90 degrees right. The Mk 8** was propelled by a burner-cycle combustion engine fuelled by shale oil and compressed air and could run for 4,572m (5,000 yards) at 45.5 knots. The warhead comprised a substantial 805lb of Torpex and could cut a destroyer in half.

The last Second World War–designed submarine in the Royal Navy – HMS *Alliance* on display at the Royal Navy Submarine Museum at Gosport. She is in very bad condition externally and has deteriorated alarmingly in recent years. (World Copyright 2012 Peter C. Smith)

They carried twenty torpedoes with six reloads carried for the internal bow tubes and four for the stern tubes. As minelayers they could carry a total of eighteen Mark V M2 mines. They also had a single 10.2cm (4-inch)/40 calibre quick-firing Mk XXIII gun built in a shielded mounting ahead of the conning tower on a S2 mounting and later a twin 20mm Mark 12A Oerlikon AA gun was carried for a short period. They had a crew of five officers and fifty-six ratings.

Once her delayed introduction into service commenced on 9 October 1947 the first voyage made by *Alliance* was a month-long experimental cruise down through the Atlantic Ocean to the coast of Africa to test the Snorkel gear. She remained submerged for thirty days not surfacing again until 8 November, which proved the efficiency of this equipment.

In the autumn of 1951 the *Alliance* was despatched to Canada to assist in anti-submarine warfare (ASW) training, arriving at Halifax, Nova Scotia on 11 September. On 19 May 1954 the *Alliance* became the flagship of Admiral Sir Michael Denny, the Commander-in-Chief Home Fleet and, later, of Rear Admiral G. B. H. Fawkes, Commander Submarine Force Eastern Atlantic.

Following more than a decade of operations the *Alliance* was taken in hand in 1958 for an two-year modernisation, with all exterior fitments like the external tubes, the deck gun etc completely taken away to free her hull of all encumbrances, and her conning tower was replaced by an aluminium 'sail' or 'fin' some 7.924m (26ft 6in) tall which enclosed all her masts. This streamlining was to improve underwater speed but only resulted in a slight improvement, from 8 knots to 10 knots. However, the access hatch for the gun was retained, and later utilised once more when she embarked a gun when serving in Far Eastern waters. The changes resulted in her normal surface/submerged tonnage being altered to 1,385/1,620 tons and her length increased to 85.77m (281ft 4.75in). Her Tactical Command System (Submarine) (TCS (S)) was a Mark 2,

mod.2, she carried 120 RD and 138F Asdic UT/E 267 Pulse Width (PW) radar.

The *Alliance* went out to the Far East and while on that station was reported to have tested a new camouflage paint scheme. She returned to home waters and on 13 January 1968 ran herself aground on a rocky ledge off the Isle of Wight and was embarrassingly stuck there for the best part of three days. No great damage was done, however, other than to pride. On 5 November 1968 the *Alliance* took part in a major NATO exercise held in the eastern Mediterranean, EDEN APPLE which lasted until the 20th.

On 29 September 1971, while berthed alongside at Portland, due to a fault in her ventilation system which permitted a build-up of hydrogen,

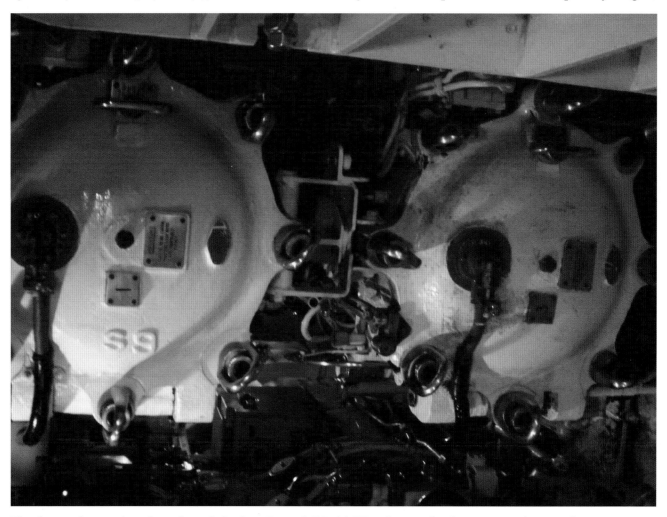

The forward torpedo-tubes aboard the last Second World War-designed submarine in the Royal Navy – HMS *Alliance* on display at the Royal Navy Submarine Museum at Gosport. (World Copyright 2012 Peter C. Smith)

a fatal battery explosion took place on board. She suffered one fatality and fourteen of her crew were injured. Full details have never been released. She remained accident-prone and, on 1 February 1972 while making a test dive off Plymouth, her engine room flooded and she bounced off the seabed at a depth of 37.185m (122ft). It later transpired that she had been making too steep a diving angle because of incorrect trimming to compensate for the flooding. With the arrival of the much-improved Porpoise- and Oberon-class conventional submarines she was taken out of service. She never served as a submarine again, being decommissioned and for six years from 1973 was utilised as a static training vessel replacing the smaller submarine *Tabard* at the Royal Navy Submarine base HMS *Dolphin* at Gosport. In August 1979, it having been decided to retain her as a museum ship, she was taken under tow to Southampton to have her keel strengthened. This was because she was to be preserved mounted on concrete cradles and totally out of the water.

One unique event that took place down the years was a series of recordings made aboard her by the Composer Marvin Ayres in 2011. As part of his Sacred Spaces concept Ayres played cellos, violins and violas in the confined space of the submarine and recorded the resulting echoes, reverberations and other feedback in the restricted metal space for an ethereal and distinctly different sound range.

Over the years she deteriorated badly from rust corrosion and neglect with gaping holes which have become pigeon roosts! When I visited her in November 2011 she was in a bad way externally. She clearly needs considerable money to be spent on her and, as a start, a £1.5 million contract has been awarded to Balfour Beatty Regional Civil Engineering to install a sheet-piled cofferdam around her, which will be infilled so that much-needed restoration work can commence. The *Alliance* was awarded a total of £3.4 million from the Heritage Lottery Fund grant to replace the bow and stern sections that have been allowed to so badly rust away. The 'Saving HMS *Alliance* Appeal' hopes to pull in more funds to aid this work. Viewing platforms, the opening up of the sail and a visitor gallery are among projected improvements.

As the last survivor of her class, *Alliance* was transferred on permanent loan from the Royal Navy and became a museum ship and memorial in 1981. She serves as an open memorial most fitting to remember the 4,334 British submariners who gave their lives in the two world wars and the 739 who were lost in peacetime submarine disasters.

The *Alliance* can be found at the Royal Navy Submarine Museum, Haslar Jetty Road, Gosport, Hants, PO12 2AS. Tel: 0239 252 9217. e-mail admin@rnsubmus.co.uk.

GREAT BRITAIN

The *Great Britain* is truly a unique vessel and most worthy of preservation. When built at Bristol during the years 1839 to 1844, she incorporated an impressive number of original features and innovations as befits her designer's towering design flair and engineering ambition. Her chief claims to such fame were that she was the first ocean-going vessel to be built of iron; that she was the first large ship to be fitted with a screw propeller, six bladed; and that at the time she was by far and away the largest ship afloat. More than all these notable 'firsts' she was also the first ship to be built with a double bottom, transverse watertight bulkheads, folding masts and a semi-balanced rudder. Little wonder then that HRH The Duke of Edinburgh was to write that the *Great Britain* 'represents a vital stage in that revolution (from sail to power) and is therefore of immense interest to future generations'.

All these extraordinary new concepts were combined by the brilliance of that towering genius Isambard Kingdom Brunel into a vessel which set

The SS *Great Britain* with ornamental scroll work and coat of arms. (Photo by Mandy Reynolds, reproduced by courtesy of Great Western Dockyard, Bristol)

The impressive stern work of the SS *Great Britain* in dock at Bristol. (Photo by David Noton, reproduced by courtesy of Great Western Dockyard, Bristol)

The SS *Great Britain* in her special dock at the Great Western Dockyard, Bristol. (Photo by David Noton, reproduced by courtesy of Great Western Dockyard, Bristol)

the whole pattern for the new age in shipping which has lasted to the present day. She is the only survivor of those early iron merchant ships and was the first and the finest. From the embryo design as represented by the *Great Britain*, this nation led the world in marine engineering and British ships and shipbuilders became pre-eminent until the 1930s. The dramatic effect of the *Great Britain* and her successors on the North Atlantic passenger trade can be gauged by the comparison of sail and steam vessels on this, the world's busiest shipping route, in 1858 and 1860. Whereas at the first period there were some 138 sailing ships plying between Britain and Quebec and only nineteen steamers, within just two years there were thirty-seven steamers on the route.

The first regular trans-Atlantic route was established in 1816 and for many years it was American dominated. It was Brunel's early creation, the giant *Great Western*, that first challenged this dominance in 1837, but she proved too expensive to maintain the challenge. Thus it was that in March 1839 the Great Western Steamship Company announced that they were to undertake the building of a superior craft, to be named *City of New York*. She was originally to have been a paddle steamer, as was the *Great Western*, but this design was altered during her building, as was, fortunately for posterity, her name.

A design committee was formed consisting of Brunel himself, Captain Claxton, Thomas Guppy and William Patterson. Trials were held on the screw schooner *Archimedes*, with members of the committee aboard, which led to the recommendation that this system be adopted for the *Great Britain* and, instead of tendering out her contract, the company prepared to construct her themselves. Accordingly, a site at Wapping Wharf, Bristol, was purchased and the existing dry-dock enlarged.

The construction of such a radical machine called into being whole new skills with the traditional functions of the shipwrights being happily married to the newer skills of the boilermakers in a system that also endured, with modifications, to the present day. As completed she was indeed an impressive vessel. Her length was 98.156m (322ft)

and her beam 15.392m (50.5ft). Her tonnage was 3,270 and her cost £117,295. Her main propulsion was an engine developing 600hp giving her a maximum speed under power alone of 12.5 knots. Her fuel capacity was 1,200 tons of coal. She carried masting that was wire rigged, having a mainmast and five auxiliary masts to complement her single funnel. She had a crew of 130 officers and men and first-class passenger accommodation for 360 which included thirty-six staterooms with single beds and 113 staterooms with two beds.

The *Great Britain* was floated out at a launching ceremony attended by Prince Albert on 19 July 1843 and she was finally completed the following April. Trials were held that winter and, on their successful completion, the ship was formally registered on 14 January 1845. Her maiden voyage was to London where she remained for five months and was inspected by Queen Victoria in April 1845. In June she left for Liverpool from which port she sailed on her first North Atlantic crossing to New York on 26 July. This first passage took fourteen days, twenty-one hours, at an average speed of 9.25 knots and, on her arrival in New York on 10 August, she received a resounding reception.

Subsequent voyages in heavy weather revealed some construction weaknesses in the ship and she consequently underwent a complete overhaul at Liverpool during the spring of 1856 when the six-bladed propeller was replaced by a four-bladed one and one mast was removed.

The next North Atlantic crossing by the *Great Britain* reduced her passage time to 13.5 days but her fifth crossing was a disaster for, on 22 September, she ran aground in Dundrum Bay, Ireland. Her salvage was protracted and she did not finally arrive back at Liverpool until the following August. Her repair bill could not be met by the Great Western Company and in 1850 she was sold. This marked the end of her Atlantic days and proved the death blow to the Great Western Company which was wound up soon afterward.

The *Great Britain* was now taken in hand and completely refitted for the Australian run. She was equipped with new engines and re-boilered

The bows of the SS *Great Britain* with ornamental scroll work and coat of arms. (Photo by Mandy Reynolds, reproduced by courtesy of Great Western Dockyard, Bristol)

The impressive masting arrangement and funnel of the SS *Great Britain*.
(Courtesy of Richard Pope, Great Western Dockyard, Bristol)

and a third propeller, three-bladed this time, was fitted to her. Twin funnels were also built and her masting was changed yet again to become two foremasts, a square-rigged mast and one of the original mizzen masts. A deckhouse was added and the dining saloon converted into extra cargo space. She could then carry 730 passengers and their baggage to the Antipodes. Her first voyage to this new destination commenced in August 1852 when she carried 650 passengers and a cargo of gold and sterling. This voyage was also beset with disaster for she ran short of fuel over 1,126.54km (700 miles) out from Table Bay, South Africa, and had to put back there to replenish. She finally reached Melbourne with a journey time of eighty-two days. Compare this with the *Cutty Sark* earlier and it can be seen why the steamship took some time to become established.

Yet another extensive refit followed and she continued on the Australia run, making a total of thirty-two round trips over the next fifteen years, including trooping trips to the Crimea and India, but when she returned to Liverpool in February 1876 she was laid up and offered for sale with no takers for several years. Finally, in 1882, she was sold to Anthony Gibbs and again was overhauled and refitted as a cargo carrier with a capacity of 3,000 tons of bulk cargo. She made two trips from Liverpool to San Francisco via the Cape with cargoes of coal, returning laden with wheat.

Once more, however, her persistent ill-luck dogged her and on her third such voyage she ran into a gale off Cape Horn. She was still trying to round the Horn a month later when a fire damaged one of her cargo holds and she had to put into the Falkland Islands for repair. The

View of the ship's galley with authentic kitchen utensils aboard the SS *Great Britain*, Bristol. (Photo by Paul Blakemore, reproduced by courtesy of Great Western Dockyard, Bristol)

The dining room laid for Christmas luncheon aboard the SS *Great Britain* at Bristol. (Photo by Stephen Lewis, reproduced by courtesy of Great Western Dockyard, Bristol)

resources of the Falklands were too meagre to enable this to be done and the same year, 1886, she was listed as a constructive total loss and sold to the Falkland Islands Company as a wool and coal storage hulk, a sad fate for so famous and revolutionary a ship. In this lowly capacity she remained on those lonely shores for twenty-seven years, her bunkers helping to re-coal the battle-cruisers *Inflexible* and *Invincible* which enabled them to destroy the German Admiral von Spee's squadron at the Battle of the Falkland Islands in 1914.

When her decks finally rotted away and her days, even as a storage hulk, were over, she was towed across to Sparrow Cove just north of Port Stanley and scuttled when initial efforts at saving her had failed. It was not until 1966 that interest was revived and then not by Britain by an

American concern, the Pacific Bridge and Engineering Company of San Francisco. Their President, William Swigert Jnr, was interested in the *Great Britain* as a unique vessel and carried out extensive surveys of her with a view to exhibiting her. The Brunel Society of Great Britain decided in 1968 that a salvage feasibility study should be undertaken and on 4 May 1968 a historic meeting took place in Bristol between these two parties and representatives of the National Maritime Museum, the Society of Nautical Research and Messrs Burness, Corlett and Partners. Due to the overriding importance the vessel held in Britain's maritime history, Mr Swigert agreed to pool his knowledge and support the *Great Britain* Project which was launched.

The committee was formed under the chairmanship of Richard Goold-Adams and set about raising funds. Once sufficient initial response had been obtained (which included a gift of £150,000 from Mr Jack Hayward, the saviour of Lundy Island for the nation) a full survey was made of the old vessel. Negotiations with the Governor of the Falkland Islands resulted in the release of the ship to the Project Committee and the salvage was entrusted to Risdon Beazley Limited of Southampton. The *Great Britain* was refloated and towed into a submersible pontoon. The ocean tug *Varius II* then towed the ship in the pontoon for the 7,600-mile journey to her home port of Bristol where she finally arrived in July 1970.

The *Great Britain* was docked in the very dock in which she had originally been built and the work of preservation and restoration got under way. The Company had a programme mapped out over a decade which included the following stages of restoration to her original appearance in 1843 and had plans to rebuild enough of her interior to enable the visitor to visualise what life aboard her was like in her heyday. This restoration work included the provision of six masts, the funnel and deck fittings, the restoration of the first-class public rooms in the stern part of the ship and six cabins complete with fittings. A facsimile of the ship's engines and original six-bladed propeller were constructed and the officers' and crew's quarters restored.

By September 1973 her bows had been almost completely restored and the bowsprit was in place, together with the figurehead and trailboards in their original colours. Her decks were planked over, thus making her weatherproof. The design of her figurehead was that of the Royal Coat of Arms flanked by a golden lion and unicorn, while the trailboards had on them symbols of the arts and the trades. Along her hull the imitation gun ports were also finely painted in. This work cost £320,000 over ten years and was to have been completed by 1984. Even by 1974 some 90,000 visitors had gone aboard her at the Great Western Dock, Gas Gerry Road, Bristol. In 2005 the ship was given dehumidifiers to preserve the hull and her dock was given a waterline sheet of glass plate as well. Nowadays visitor totals have increased to 170,000 and the vessel is listed as part of the National Historic Fleet, Core Collection. The *Great Britain* Exhibition has been given numerous prestigious awards including the IStruckE Award in 2006; the Gulbenkian Prize the same year and the European Museum of the Year Award's Micheletti Prize in 2007.

BALMORAL

The steam-driven paddle steamer *Balmoral* was built in 1949 and replaced an earlier vessel of the same name which had served the Red Funnel fleet since 1900. The old vessel had been built by S. McKnight at Ayr Shipyard, Scotland, being their Yard No. 60, and her engines were supplied by Hutson & Son. She was launched for the Southampton Isle of Wight & South of England Royal Mail Steam Packet Company on Tuesday 15 May 1900 and she had a gross tonnage of 473, a length of 71.932m (236ft) and a 8.236m (27.1ft) beam. During the course of her long and distinguished career the old *Balmoral* had been requisitioned by the Royal Navy to serve in both world wars, the first period between May 1915 and June 1919 as a minesweeper, while during the Second World War she was fitted out as an anti-aircraft vessel between 1940 and 1946, surviving both stints of front-line duty. By 1949 she was worn out and was scrapped at Northam's shipbreaking yard.

Her successor was a different vessel altogether, being a motor vessel of 688 gross tonnage, with an overall length of 62.03m (203½ft) and a beam

The paddle steamer *Balmoral* passing the Clifton suspension bridge on the river Avon near Bristol. (Copyright and Courtesy of *Waverley* Excursions Ltd)

A starboard bow photograph of the paddle steamer *Balmoral* with a full complement of passengers and dressed overall. (Copyright and Courtesy of *Waverley* Excursions Ltd)

of 9.75m (32ft). She was built at the Woolston yard of John I. Thornycroft & Company, better known for producing fast destroyers, and was launched on 27 June 1949. Her original engines were 6-cylinder 600bhp, two-stroke Newbury Sirron diesels. Her owners, the Red Funnel Line, operated her mainly as a ferry ship between Southampton and Cowes, IoW (she had a capacity of ten vehicles on her rear deck), although she did undertake some coastal excursion work up until 1968.

In that year the *Balmoral* was declared redundant; custom-built car ferries of much higher capacity had long since replaced her and she was deemed too old. She was sold to P. & A. Campbell who operated her in their White Funnel Fleet based at Bristol for a further twenty-two years. For a brief period the *Balmoral* was moved to Dundee and converted into a floating restaurant, but this venture did not work out and she was put up for sale once more.

Now classed as a coastal excursion vessel after undergoing an extensive renovation, her former car deck was converted into an enclosed and heated passenger lounge, which gave her a passenger capacity of about 750. She also had a restaurant, two bars, and a gift shop installed. In 2002–03 the *Balmoral* underwent another major renovation, partly financed from the Heritage Lottery Fund, the principal upgrade being the replacement of her old engines with new 4-stroke engines built in Denmark by A/S Grenaa Motofabrik, which run at higher speeds with 4,000hp more power. She had a new gearbox by Reintjes GmbH, Hameln, Germany and new propellers from Stone Marine, Singapore. This involved the removal of the funnel and its later reinstatement, along with a new funnel cowl. The work was carried out by Avonmouth Ship Repairers at Bristol and the promenade deck was also refitted. On completion of this work on 30 May 2003 she made a new inaugural cruise from the Isle of Man. In 2004 it

The paddle steamer *Balmoral* (left) along with her current teammate, the *Waverley*. (Copyright and Courtesy of *Waverley* Excursions Ltd)

was the turn of the dining saloon to be considerably upgraded.

More recently, in November 2010, the *Balmoral* benefitted from a grant from the ITV Peoples Millions project to further refurbish and upgrade the Britannia Lounge and bar. The *Balmoral* is currently owned by the Waverley Steam Navigation Company Ltd and operated by Waverley Excursions, being based in the Bristol Channel since 1986 and carrying the IMO 5034927. She works in conjunction with the paddle steamer *Waverley* and the pair cover most areas of the south and western English coasts of the United Kingdom during the summer months with trips farther afield to the Isle of Man, Scotland and Northern Ireland.

She has now far exceeded the longevity of her predecessor, having celebrated her sixtieth anniversary with a special cruise on 27 June 2009, which circumnavigated the Isle of Wight.

ALBION

The Norfolk trading wherry was, in living memory, as familiar a part of the traditional Broadland scene as the windmill. Now, however, both have gone, save for a few lonely survivors and the Broads themselves have passed from serene and peaceful unspoilt waterways to a hurly-burly, crowded holiday area with little of its blissful calm and isolation remaining. At their peak, around the turn of the twentieth century, the Norfolk wherries abounded as a form of bulk cargo carrier along the shallow rivers and inlets of the Norfolk and Suffolk Broads.

These craft really derive from the older Norfolk keels which performed a similar function on these rivers from medieval times to around the early 1800s. Stepping a single mast amidships carrying a square sail, they plied between the Broadland towns taking wheat and kindred cargoes down to Great Yarmouth, returning with coal, timber and other bulky cargoes. The word wherry is an ancient one and was originally used as a general term for a small, fast, oared craft principally for the transportation of passengers and light goods.

It is uncertain exactly when the transition from keel to wherry took place but at some time during the late eighteenth century the shipwrights adapted the double-ended hull of the small passenger-carrying wherry and stepped the mast up in the

The wherry *Albion* makes a fine sight on the Norfolk Broads. (Copyright & Courtesy The Norfolk Wherry Trust)

eyes of the ship and rigged her with a large fore-and-aft mainsail. The result was the now traditional form of Norfolk trading wherry, combining as it does the superior handling qualities of a passenger wherry with the cargo carrying capacity of the Norfolk keel and featuring a long unencumbered hold of some 10.668m (35ft) or more. Certainly in terms of handiness and speed this new sail bulk carrier compared more than favourably with the keel and largely supplanted it within a very short period, Today there are no keels at all in existence and only from old photographs can their lines be made out.

It was at this stage also that the development of the canal was providing a boom in inland waterway transport and between 1790 and 1810 the three main Norfolk rivers were extensively re-developed with locks and channels which gave practical transportation routes from Great Yarmouth down to Beccles and Bungay on the Waveney, to North Walsham and Stalham via the river Ant and to Aylsham on the Upper Bure. It is often forgotten just how extensive the old Broadland system used to be, and many of these old abandoned river routes might again come to life as a result of the ever increasing overcrowding problems on the present area of the Broads as utilised by pleasure craft today.

The heyday of the Norfolk trading wherry was between 1850 and 1900 and on one famous occasion no less than sixty-one wherries crossed the Breydon Water on the same tide having been wind-bound by prolonged gales. For their cargoes, they carried timber and logs, bricks, fertilizers, grain and flour. They trans-shipped coal at Great Yarmouth out at sea which proved their hardiness. Indeed, their trade could be summed up in the phrase 'corn and coal' for these were the basic cargoes until supplemented in latter years by sugar beet. As with other sail-powered craft, the widespread introduction of the motor lorry finally brought about their demise and the 200 or more wherries at the turn of the century were reduced to a mere thirty or so by 1930.

During the opening up of the Broads to pleasure craft at the beginning of the twentieth century an adaptation of the standard wherry was made to make the pleasure wherry, by which normal trading wherries were transformed during the summer months to spacious houseboats, reverting to normal trade in the autumn and winter months. Also introduced was the wherry yacht, which was not a true wherry at all but a wherry-rigged barge yacht, carvel built.

The true trading wherry was quite distinctive with its large black sail, black from the dressing of herring oil and tar, and its great black hull, a sombre vessel relieved only by the splash of colour at the mast-head where the owners had their own distinctive colour bands or house colours painted up. The great mainsail was high peaked to catch every scrap of wind from the low-lying and tree-fringed Broadland rivers, and the Norfolk wherry was the last sailing craft to feature the bonnet, which, when laced on, quickly added another 0.609m (2ft) to the sail area. When the wind failed these great black boats were quanted along with 7.315m (24ft) poles with splayed feet to prevent them sinking into the ooze. The other outstanding feature of the wherry was the single unstayed pole mast, set in a tabernacle, so finely balanced that it could be raised with ease by a single man or boy.

With the passing of the wherry during the Second World War these unique craft appeared doomed but, in 1949, there was founded the Norfolk Wherry Trust, when a small group of far-sighted individuals got together with the intention of acquiring one or more examples of a trading wherry under sail for the sake of posterity. The ship they managed to find and preserve is the famous old *Albion*.

She had originally been built by one Billy Brighton at Lake Lothing, on the seaward side of the lock at Oulton Broad and is not typical in that she was carvel-built in order, it is believed, to prevent damage to her hull while passing through the three locks of the Waveney Navigation. She was built for W.D. & A.E. Walker, the maltsters of Bungay, in 1898. Nowadays she carries a lowerable 12.80m (42-ft) mast. She later served with the fleet of Reckitt & Coleman under the name *Plane* and for many years was used by them as a mustard store. When restored it was hoped to keep her in trade, but, despite valiant efforts for two years, this proved impossible.

A fine bow view of the wherry *Albion* with her huge black sail at full extension. (Copyright & Courtesy The Norfolk Wherry Trust)

The Trust however, did not give up and the *Albion* has been largely rebuilt and re-equipped. In 1967 a new sail was made and a year later a new mast stepped, both presented through the generosity of local well-wishers. In 1969 when seventy years old, her timbers were renewed, all parts treated with fungicides and her interior adapted for passenger accommodation. Her

Period fittings and fixtures below decks aboard the Norfolk Wherry *Albion* (Copyright & Courtesy The Norfolk Wherry Trust)

upkeep was mainly paid for by the 700 members of the Trust and by those actively using her for venture holidays, mainly school groups who took her out under an experienced master for summer cruises along the waterways she had traded for so many years. As such she is now safe for future generations to enjoy, to the delight of all who love the Broads and the interest of all marine historians and lovers of sail. When I was invited aboard

to inspect her in 1974 she was in fine condition and moored at Houghton Mill, near St Ives in Cambridgeshire.

Currently the *Albion* is fully restored for pleasure sailing with twelve berths and is based at Horsefen Road, Womack Water, near Ludham, Norfolk. Her postal address is Forsythe Wherry Yard, Horsefen Road, Ludham, Norfolk, NR29 5QG. Tel: 01692 501 094.

LYDIA EVA

The herring industry once made the Norfolk port of Great Yarmouth one of the premier fishing ports in the world. The whole area was geared to this tremendous industry and it has been estimated that each boat at work meant the employment of 100 people, the fishermen, boat-builders, net-makers, the fisher-girls, the market officials, a huge industry and a booming one. This heyday was reached in 1913 with more than 1,000 fishing boats based at Great Yarmouth alone. This flourishing trade was devastated during the Great War when a large part of the foreign market was cut off and boats or their men were requisitioned for war duties. In 1918 the coming of peace failed to restore the situation because the nations lacked the funds to purchase herring in the great pre-war quantities, and foreign nations began to construct their own fleets. The herring stock had also been grossly over-fished and went into a rapid decline. The result was a steady decline in the Norfolk fishing fleet until, in 1969, no boats arrived in the port at all.

The best known of the various types of vessels used in this industry were the little steam drifters which once clustered so thickly around the quaysides at Great Yarmouth and Lowestoft in Suffolk. The *Lydia Eva* was built in 1930 by King's Lynn Slipway Company as one of the last acts of faith by a local owner in the future of his dying trade. She proved to be the last vessel built there and when launched was towed round to Great Yarmouth to be fitted out.

The *Lydia Eva* was steel built and had a triple-expansion boiler featuring natural draught only and was designed to utilise both trawl and drift-net fishing methods. She was owned by Harry Eastwick of Gorleston. The vessel had a tonnage of 138 GRT, was 20m (95ft) long with a beam of 6.3m (20.6ft) and a draught of 3m (9.8ft); was powered by a Crabtree triple-expansion engine and had a crew of ten men. *The Lydia Eva* (YH89) underwent her sea trials on 22 July 1930.

The *Lydia Eva* commenced work at once and her record catch, achieved in 1937, was 220,000 herring, a season's record. Although embodying the then latest developments of the trade, she was only in service for eight years before being put up for sale, and, after a final catch being landed in December 1938, *Lydia Eva* and the rest of the Eastwick flotilla was sold to Norford Sufflings who sold her on to Geoffrey Banes of the Caernarvonshire Yacht Company in 1939.

On the outbreak of war she was contracted to the Royal Air Force and, following some conversion work, was used as a target tug, danlayer and other similar duties all around the coast. Her owners became Western Marine Craft where she was managed by J. Deheer on behalf of the Air Ministry. On 10 December 1942 the Ministry of War Transport requisitioned her for the Admiralty for £50 and she was used by the Ministry of Aircraft Production for salvage work which continued until 1947. Under their ownership she was converted as a cargo carrier with a derrick for loading and unloading dan buoys and markers; in this guise she worked by Abersoch, Anglesey. During the subsequent years her base shifted down the Welsh coast to Pwellheli, then to Ilfracombe and by 1945 she was working from Maryport, Cumbria before moving south once more to Weymouth. On 1 April 1947 the *Lydia Eva* was sold to the Air Ministry as a mooring vessel and they renamed her *Watchmoor*. Her career proved equally diverse and between 1947 and 1965 she was based for various periods at Milford Haven, Watchet in Somerset, Appledore in north Devon, London, Cardiff, Pembroke Dock and Whitehaven in Cumbria. On

A stern view of the *Lydia Eva*, now moored up as a Museum to the East Coast Fishing Industry, on the River Yare at Great Yarmouth.
(Copyright & Courtesy of Ashley Dace)

1 April 1961 the Marine Services Division of the Royal Navy took over the *Watchmoor*, equipping her with a new Stockton Chemical Engineers and Riley Boilers Ltd, RT Scotch boiler and an improved wheelhouse, with improved Marconi electronics and she was painted Navy grey, but this expense had just been incurred when yet further problems arose. The *Lydia Eva* suffered engine failure in 1966 and had to be towed into Holyhead by the *Empire Netta*. She was surveyed again in September 1966 and found not to be worth any further expense and so the following year found her employed as a plane-guard until the minesweeper *Invermoriston* and then the *Miner III* replaced her. A boiler clean followed in December 1967 and the following January she was working at Clovelly, north Devon. This proved to be her last official duty and in 1968 she was stripped of her navigation equipment and with just two years' intermittent service, most of it in dockyard hands, she was put up for sail by them at Milford Haven docks.

Her long service with the various official agencies had at least ensured that she had survived when many similar fishing vessels had been making their last sad journeys to the breakers' yard. Even so, she would most likely have joined them there but for the activities of the Maritime Trust who purchased her, restored her original name and took her to Milford Haven in 1971, where, after undergoing a comprehensive survey and docking at Holman & Sons yard, Penzance, she was found to be in excellent condition. She steamed round to Great Yarmouth, arriving on 1 October 1972, an operation which called into play skills of engine handling and boiler fuelling almost lost to modern seamen, but it was accomplished very successfully.

Restoration work then began at a Lowestoft shipyard. Her engine was retained and her boilers were re-tubed and a new wheelhouse was fitted by Overys. The *Lydia Eva* was re-rigged as a drifter and her fish-hold was converted into a permanent exhibition room to illustrate the history of the fishing industry. She was larger than most drifters, being built at a much later period than most and, as such, was an ideal choice for preservation. She was then moored as a floating museum at South

Quay opposite the Great Yarmouth Town Hall, her old home port, and was the last link with the industry that made that town so prosperous in the days before North Sea Oil rigs, gas pipelines and wind farms dominated North Sea industries. Here she was berthed for the next five years

In 1978 the *Lydia Eva* was moved to join the Maritime Trust's national collection of ships at St Katherine's Dock hard by the Tower of London for eight years before financial difficulties forced the closure of the exhibition. She was then laid up once more in the West India Dock, almost forgotten. Her next move was made in 1990 when she returned to the east coast, a new *Lydia Eva* and *Mincarlo* Charitable Trust Limited having been

The capstan on the *Lydia Eva*, these steam-powered mechanisms were used to help haul the nets in. It was built at Beccles, not too far from Yarmouth. (Copyright and Courtesy of Ashley Dace)

set up the year before by East Anglian well-wishers and conservationists backed by the respective county councils, with the avowed aim of sharing her between the two ports of Great Yarmouth and Lowestoft. They were successful enough to enable the *Lydia Eva* to be, yet again, towed back to Great Yarmouth, on 30 June 1990 by the Port Authority tug *Hector Read*.

Another dry-docking followed at Lowestoft in 2000 which found that she was in a far worse condition than imagined with her hull rusted away dangerously. An appeal was launched to save her and the Heritage Lottery Fund was approached for aid. For many years while awaiting the £1m funding needed it was touch-and-go that she would survive and she was only kept afloat by automatic pumps that started up whenever she started leaking, which was often. Finally, the National Lottery provided £839,000 in 2007 which enabled Small and Company's Lowestoft yard to make real progress. Much of her interior wooden fittings were restored free of charge by instructors

and trainees from Lowestoft's International Boat-building Training College. A new steam engine was built for her by the Great Yarmouth firm of Crabtree, the biggest they had ever assembled, and trials conducted on Lake Lothing until finally she was ready to go to sea once more.

Currently the *Lydia Eva* alternates between the two ports, being open in the spring and summer months, lovingly maintained by volunteers and visited by many thousands of visitors and in receipt of the Small Commercial Vessels' certificate which enables her to take paying customers on short voyages.

Like the *Mincarlo, the Lydia Eva is* worked by a volunteer crew and alternates between Heritage Quay, Great Yarmouth, Norfolk and the Yacht Harbour at Lowestoft, Suffolk, where they are open to the public with free admission between Easter and October each year (closed Mondays) and are laid up during the winter months for refurbishments.

MINCARLO

In the same way that the *Lydia Eva* and the *Albion* represent the last of their breed in East Anglian maritime history, so does the Lowestoft Sidewinder Trawler *Mincarlo*. Although modern by comparison with this duo, she is still unique and it is vital that she is kept to remind us of the enormous fishing industry that once thrived in what is now an industrial backwater area of modern England and pulled in enormous catches of cod, haddock, plaice, skate and sole for the plates of Britain's families.

The *Mincarlo* was built by Brooke Marine, Lowestoft, being their Yard No. 281 and cost £76,600. She was laid down in 1960. She has a gross tonnage of 166 and a net tonnage of 56, with a length overall of 33.15m (108.75ft), a beam of 6.9m (22.7ft) and a moulded depth of 3.43m (11.25ft). She is powered by a 5-cylinder, vertical, 4-stroke cycle, naturally aspirated, AK Diesel, developing 500shp at 320revs, driving through an AK Diesel 2:1 ratio reverse reduction gearbox giving her a 160rpm propeller speed Her best

Looking forward along the deck of the trawler *Mincarlo* moored at the Historic Boat Quay. (Copyright & Courtesy of Ashley Dace)

loaded speed was 10 knots. She had a crew of eleven men.

Mincarlo was launched on 25 September 1961, one of three sister vessels (the others were *Bryher* and *Rosevear*) built for the Lowestoft firm of W. H. Podd Ltd, who bestowed on them the names of three islands in the Scillies group. She carried the registration LT412 when she first went to sea working for the Podd family, one of sixty such ships sailing regularly from Lowestoft. Her actual fishing career was comparatively brief, thirteen years in total, and she proved one of the best boats in the ever-shrinking Lowestoft fleet.

This type of fishing craft was known as side trawler, or locally as 'Sidewinders' due to their nets being warped out on the starboard side of her hull, being fed through blocks hung off gallows forward and aft, as distinct from the stern and beam trawling methods which, once in the minority, eventually totally eclipsed them. Her

hold could once contain 5,200ft^3 of fish catch, including her 690ft^3 ice room and she has a fresh water capacity of seven tons. Each of her two trawls was equipped with otter boards, which serve to automatically ensure the mouth of the net is totally open while working. The nets themselves had ground ropes, some 12m (40ft) in length, which served to keep them down on the bed of the sea and dragged across the sand flushing flatfish from their burrows.

The Podd family finally sold her to the much larger Putford Enterprises organisation who continued to work her as a fisher boat until June 1975. At the end of this time the *Mincarlo* was converted internally by Putford to serve as a standby ship to service the North Sea Oil and Gas Fields that had begun replacing fishing as the power-house of the local economy. Renamed as *Putford Merlin* in April, she was kept busy on these duties until 1989, when it was decided

A view of the small galley aboard the trawler *Mincarlo*. (Copyright & Courtesy of Ashley Dace)

that she was economically unviable and she was replaced by a purpose-built ship. Redundant and unwanted, she was moored in Lowestoft at the yard which had originally built her.

Luckily the *Lydia Eva* Trust managed to negotiate a deal which saw them take over the *Mincarlo* as partner vessel for the nominal price of £1. This organisation then became the *Lydia Eva* and *Mincarlo* Charitable Trust and began working on restoring both vessels to their former glory. Like the *Lydia Eva*, the *Mincarlo* is worked by a volunteer crew and alternates between Heritage Quay, Great Yarmouth, Norfolk and the Yacht Harbour at Lowestoft, Suffolk, where they are open to the public with free admission between Easter and October each year (closed Fridays) and are laid up during the winter months for refurbishments at Small & Co's facility. She is currently feeling her age and in need of some considerable work and, in preparation for this, she was dry-docked on 20 September 2011 for a full marine survey to be carried out.

Contact details for correspondence only is 75 Normanston Drive, Lowestoft, Suffolk, NR32 2PU. Tel: 01502 565234. web site – www.lydiaeva.org.uk. e-mail – enquiries@lydiaeva/org.uk.

UNICORN

One of the very oldest of our preserved ships is the frigate *Unicorn*. She is a unique vessel of special interest which was built on the lines of the frigate *Leda*, which herself was copied from the French frigate *Hebe*, taken as a prize by HMS *Rainbow* in 1782, according to Master Shipwright George Parkin at Chatham dockyard.

The *Unicorn* was a 46-gun, fifth-rate wooden frigate of 1,080 tons. She was built of oak in No. 4 Slipway at Chatham to the design of Sir Robert Seppings, who was Surveyor of the Navy between 1813 and 1832. Her dimensions were 58.55m (152ft 9.75in) along her gun deck, or 42.67m (140ft 9in) between perpendiculars with a keel length of 38.709m (127ft 1.5in). Her breadth was 12.192m (40ft 3in) and her main mast was 39.928m (131ft 3in) tall with a sail area of 17,254ft^2. Her burthen was 1,078 tons, rising to 1,465 tons fully stored and ready for sea. She cost £26,461 to build.

She would have been armed with twenty-eight of the long 18-pounder guns on her main deck, with two 32-pounder carronades and two 9-pounder long guns on her forecastle and on her quarter-deck would carry two more 9-pounders and a dozen 32-pounder carronades. The total weight of her guns as equipped was 80 tons 7 cwt to which a gunpowder weight of 11 tons 19 cwt and a shot weight of 45 tons 10 cwt should be added. In practice the number and disposition of her armament would have varied from that to some extent.

Her full wartime complement would have been approximately 334 officers and men, made up of her captain, five lieutenants, eight warrant officers, eight midshipmen and mates, fifty petty officers, 160 ratings, sixteen ship's boys and fifty Royal Marines. She was launched on 30 March 1824 and cost £26,461. She introduced a system of diagonal strengthening straps of thick iron, which were fixed to the inside of her hull and produced a far more rigid structure than hitherto. This was an innovation and one that was greatly to facilitate warship construction when, soon afterwards, they had to carry the extra weights of engines and boilers. She was also fitted with iron knees, which strengthened the curved side frames and deck beams and she had a fully planked and framed bow and stern, which reduced the effects of end-on fire into the ship.

At the time she was completed the Napoleonic Wars had ended and the beginning of the *Pax Britannica* begun, when the Royal Navy, un-challenged in size, tradition and expertise, policed the world's seaways, eliminated piracy and slavery and oversaw the expansion of Empire. However, there were no immediate calls on *Unicorn* to fulfil her original function, and instead of embarking her masts, sails and rigging, she was instead, roofed over and placed in reserve until she was required. That call was destined never to come. The *Unicorn* was roofed over to preserve her until needed and in this condition lay 'in ordinary' at Chatham, Sheerness and Woolwich for many years, being used for a time as a powder ship. It was not until 5 November 1873 that she sailed for Dundee to replace the *Brilliant* as the RNR drill ship there. In her capacity as a training ship she was fitted with a single 22.86cm (9-inch), 100-pounder smooth-bore gun, and a 16.51cm (6.5-inch) 30-pounder, four 64-pounders and four 32-pounders, all for use purely in a training role. She commissioned in this capacity on 1 January 1874 and on 1 April 1906 she came under the command of the Clyde Division but remained in Dundee. When the East Scottish Division of the RNVR was formed in 1926, the *Unicorn* became its headquarters ship, and later stayed with the Tay Division, afterwards coming under

The frigate *Unicorn* (temporarily known as *Cressy* when the aircraft-carrier of the same name was in service from 1943 to 1959) is one of the oldest preserved warships in the world. She is preserved at Dundee. (World Copyright 1974, 2012 Peter C. Smith)

the control of the RNR when the Reserves were combined.

During both world wars the *Unicorn* served as the base ship of the Senior Naval Officer, Dundee. In 1939 a new aircraft carrier was built, and named HMS *Unicorn*, and during her lifespan, which included work in the invasion of Salerno, Italy in 1943, in the Indian Ocean and the Pacific in 1944–45 against the Japanese, and later during the Korean War, the old *Unicorn* was re-named as *Unicorn II*. The carrier was broken up in 1959 and the frigate, which by then had became the *Cressy*, reverted to her original name.

In 1961 the Admiralty were notified that the Earl Grey Dock, which had been *Unicorn*'s home since 1873, was to be filled in to facilitate the construction of the Tay Road Bridge, and it was decided that she could not be moved and must be scrapped. In 1962 Captain J. C. L. Anderson RNR enlisted the aid of Captain Lord Reith of

The splendid figurehead of the frigate *Unicorn* in the Victoria Dock at Dundee. (World Copyright 2012 Peter C. Smith)

Stonehaven RNVR in saving the *Unicorn*. Lord Reith approached the then First Lord of the Admiralty, Lord Carrington PC, and he decided that the *Unicorn* should be saved. On 13 November 1962, therefore, *Unicorn* shifted berth to the Camperdown Dock, later moving again to her present berth in the Victoria Dock, and continued to serve as RNR Headquarters Ship.

No sooner had this threat to her existence been overcome than a new one loomed up. Admiralty

The *Condor* anchor, on exhibit alongside the frigate *Unicorn* at Dundee's Victoria Dock. (World Copyright 1974, 2012 Peter C. Smith)

policy had been to transfer all RNR Divisions to shore establishments and in 1967 work commenced on the Tay Division's new headquarters, HMS *Camperdown*. It was at this time that the movement to preserve the old frigate commenced. Captain W. R. Stewart RNR, then the CO of the Tay Division, spoke to Vice Admiral Sir David Gregory, who suggested contacting the Earl of Dalhousie. As a result the Unicorn Preservation Society was formed to preserve the ship and use her for youth and sea training. On 26 September HRH Prince Philip, Duke of Edinburgh, accepted the *Unicorn* on behalf of the Unicorn Preservation Society, and Rear Admiral B. C. G. Place VC, Admiral Commanding Reserves, made a presentation of £5,000 to the Society as a grant in aid of the ship's future upkeep. HMS *Unicorn* then went out of commission after some 144 years' service in the Royal Navy and became Frigate *Unicorn*.

At the time the *Unicorn* was unrigged and covered over but she was in excellent condition thanks to her original roof, which she still retained, and the Society had every hope of re-rigging her and taking her to sea again. She is currently the sixth oldest ship in her original, intact, condition still existing in the world and marks the unique transitory period between sail and steam-powered vessels. However, in recent years it became clear that she was deteriorating rapidly and that the best way to preserve her for the future and protect her from the ravages of the weather was to dock her in a dry and covered berth, the preferred option being the Central Waterfront area where she could be closer to Dundee's other historical maritime treasure, the *Discovery*, as well as the V&A Dundee. To much regret, in 2008 the Heritage Lottery Fund rejected support for this proposition. A new bid is planned for 2014 in the face of increased parsimony from central government and *Unicorn* is yet another valuable relic of our naval past that lies under severe threat. *Unicorn's* future is, therefore, still in doubt. A previous vessel of the name was the flagship of the Scottish Navy and the *Unicorn* is a heraldic supporter of the Scottish Royal Arms as well as the British Royal Family, making her symbolism doubly apt.

On the quay beside *Unicorn's* berth is the *Condor* anchor. This anchor originally belonged to HMS *Brilliant* which was a contemporary frigate and *Unicorn's* predecessor at Dundee as RNR drillship from 1863 to 1872. When *Brilliant* was towed to Inverness in 1872 her anchor was landed and left behind with *Unicorn*. When *Unicorn* herself shifted berth the old anchor was handed over to HMS *Condor*, the Royal Naval Air Station at Arbroath, where it adorned the entrance for many years. The Naval Air Station was closed down in the late 1960s and taken over by the Royal Marines who decided that they no longer wanted the anchor. It was then offered once more to the *Unicorn* and accepted. Now named the *Condor* anchor, a more correct title would have been the *Brilliant* anchor. It weights over four tons and is of wrought-iron construction. The original stock, which was of wood, has been replaced with one of sheet metal.

DISCOVERY

The name *Discovery* has always been associated with voyages of exploration and the present vessel is thought to be the sixth ship to carry that name. It would not be inappropriate to mention some of her forebears and their achievements. The English East India Company was formed early in the seventeenth century and one of their first duties was the preparation of a sturdy ship named *Discovery* whose task was to penetrate the newly discovered Hudson Strait in Canada. She duly sailed for those waters in 1602 and, under the command of Captain George Weymouth, followed the Strait for a hundred leagues before the ship's company lost faith and persuaded him that they must turn back.

The discoverer himself, Sir Henry Hudson, from whom both the Bay and Strait are named, re-commissioned the *Discovery* for his fourth voyage to those regions in an attempt to find the North-West passage to the Indies. On entering the Strait and Bay the crew mutinied and turned back, setting Hudson and his officers adrift to die a lonely death. Despite this calculated callousness and cowardly behaviour, the mutineers remained unpunished when they sailed the *Discovery* back to England. The ship herself later redeemed her name by making further penetrations of those forbidding waters.

A century and a half later another *Discovery* was named; she was a small collier which had been bought by the Admiralty. She accompanied Captain James Cook when he made his last trip to the Pacific in the *Resolution.* In 1791–95 yet another collier was re-named as *Discovery* and sailed on the expedition mounted to circumnavigate the world under the command of Captain George Vancouver.

Polar exploration was the reason for the purchase of the next vessel of this name. She was a strongly-built whaler, designed to penetrate just such areas and she accompanied Captain Sir George Nares' expedition toward the North Pole in 1875. Her success proved the basis on which the present *Discovery* was constructed. Although Sir James Clarke Ross had found the fringes of the Antarctic in 1829 it was not until the International Geographical Congress in 1899 at Berlin that interest was again revived in the exploration in earnest of this bleak and remote continent. The British Government, the Royal Geographical Society and the Royal Society, all combined in 1901 to launch the National Antarctic Expedition.

The aims of the expedition were not initially concerned with reaching the South Pole, their brief being merely to penetrate as far as they could and then survey by sledge teams to ascertain the depth of the covering ice cap and the types of rock beneath the surface. Equipment was loaded to enable an equally detailed examination to be made of the surrounding ocean bed and currents. The President of the Royal Geographic Society, Sir Clements Markham, supervised the raising of the necessary £100,000 needed for the expedition and the Admiralty agreed to man the ship with a crew of volunteers, the captain selected being the then Commander Robert Falcon Scott RN.

Rather than convert existing ships, as had always been done previously, it was decided to build a ship specifically for the job based on the design of the *Discovery* of 1875 but with many additional special features. The ship was constructed of oak and elm throughout. The steel of those times was not thought to be able to withstand the effects of ice for long periods while timber would ensure that she was non-magnetic, thus not interfering with the delicate instruments with which the embarked scientists would be making their detailed surveys.

Some 3.048m (10ft) longer than her predecessor, the new *Discovery* was fitted with powerful engines but also carried a barquentine rig of sail to enable her to proceed under wind power alone with her screw hoisted up out of the water to prevent drag. She carried double top-sails and those on the fore and main masts could be interchanged. The stem was so designed in strength and shape that the vessel would ride up over the ice and crush a passage through it, while the stern

The RRS *Discovery* in dock at Dundee. (Copyright and Courtesy of Allan McKever)

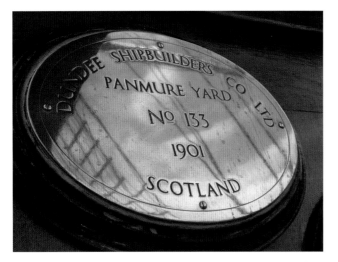

The name plate of the RRS *Discovery* showing her Dundee origins. (Copyright and Courtesy of Allan McKever)

was built overhanging to protect the screw and rudder. Her topsides were raised with specially fitted freeing scuttles in the bulwarks.

Down below the ship was laid out ready for any long period marooned in the polar ice. Lagging was fitted under the decks and the cabins were provided with double doors and skylights. Laboratories were built for the scientists and a magnetic observatory was installed with a circular space 9.144m (30ft) across and free of all metal. Sufficient stores were embarked prior to sailing to last for two years.

The *Discovery* was designed by the Admiralty's Chief Constructor, Mr W. C. Smith, and was built by the Dundee Shipbuilder Company. She had an overall length of 52.425m (172ft) at the waterline, 10.363m (34ft) beam and a displacement of 1,620 tons. She was not fitted with bilge keels through fears for her stability in ice. She was launched on 21 March 1901 by Lady Markham. Upon completion she was commissioned by her volunteer naval crew and proceeded to London where she embarked stores and her total complement of forty-three. She anchored off Cowes, Isle of Wight, in August 1901 during Cowes Week and was there inspected by the King and Queen before sailing for the Antarctic on 6 August.

On reaching New Zealand the *Discovery* was docked and a leak was repaired in her hull. During her passage she had not proved a success

under sail, being stiff and slow with a marked tendency to roll because of her lack of a bilge keel. Nevertheless she sailed from New Zealand in December 1901 to cross the world's stormiest seas fully laden. Fortunately there were no mishaps and she arrived at McMurdo Sound safely on 21 January 1902. Following a voyage along the ice barrier the *Discovery* returned here for the winter. During the summer of 1902 the various surveys were carried out but were not too successful mainly due to the inexperience of the party, only two of those embarked having worked in polar conditions before. As a result of a deep sledging penetration in the winter of 1902–03 men and dogs were exhausted, but *Discovery* had become locked into the ice and could not be freed during the summer of 1903.

The Admiralty, fearing tragedy if the *Discovery* failed to free herself, sent out a relief party in two ships and during February 1904 a passage

The king post, shrouds and belaying pins aboard the RRS *Discovery*. (Copyright and Courtesy of Allan McKever)

was blasted through the ice and she sailed free, returning to England in September of that year. Scott himself, as is well known, returned to the Antarctic eventually reaching his long-cherished goal of the South Pole, only to perish with his team on the return journey when within 17.70km (11 miles) of safety. The *Discovery* herself was put up for sale on her return, being purchased by the Hudson's Bay Company in 1905 and used by them as a trans-Atlantic store-ship before being laid up in dock in 1912. On the outbreak of the First World War she was chartered to the French Government and used by them to transport war materials by way of the Barents Sea to their Russian Allies but this traffic ceased with the collapse of Russia in anarchy in 1917 and the *Discovery* was again laid up in dock until purchased in 1923 by the *Discovery* Committee.

The Committee refitted the *Discovery* as a research ship once more and sent her out to the Antarctic again to study the habits of whales in those regions. Her voyage took her to South Georgia and Deception Island along the whaling routes. She was then commissioned to carry Sir Douglas Mawson's expedition to Australian Antarctica. A new ship was built in 1931, named *Discovery II*, and the old *Discovery* was once more laid up in the East India Dock in London. Here she lay forlornly for six years before being sold for a nominal sum to the Boy Scouts for use as a training vessel. Unfortunately this organisation proved unable to afford her upkeep and she reverted to Admiralty control in 1955 when she was commissioned as HMS *Discovery* as the Drill Ship of the London Division of the Royal Naval Reserve. In 1960 the forward part of the ship was allocated to the Royal Navy and Royal Marines as their recruiting Headquarters, a duty which she performed admirably for many years.

The *Discovery* was berthed at King's Reach on the Victoria Embankment in central London, close by Temple underground station. Here she was open to the public and proved a considerable tourist attraction, her central location ensuring a very high footfall of more than 300,000 visitors a year being shown around her. This author was given an extensive tour of her facilities. Scott's cabin was open and his bunk, settee and personal mementoes in showcases were all on display. The wardroom similarly was kept in its original state as were many of the cabins of the officers and scientists of the original expedition. The Maritime Trust took over her care in 1979, but in 1985 she became the responsibility of the Dundee Heritage Trust. She was loaded aboard the *Happy Mariner* in March 1986 and withdrawn to the River Tay. A special dock was built for her at Discovery Point, Dundee. The RRS became a Museum Ship, restored to her 1924 condition with exhibitions and artefacts devoted to British Polar exploration. Contact: Discovery Point, Discovery Quay, Dundee DD1 4XA. Tel: 01382 309060 or admin@dundee heritage.co.uk

BRITANNIA

The Royal Yacht *Britannia* was the eighty-third ship devoted to the service of the British Monarchy, and she became one of the world's most travelled ships; during her forty-three years and 334 days' proud service to Her Majesty Queen Elizabeth II she made no less than 969 overseas voyages to every part of the globe plus 272 visits to ports in the United Kingdom. The first Royal Yacht was that of King Charles II in 1660 as Great Britain celebrated her position as the leading maritime nation and the *Britannia* proved to be the last in 1997, similarly marking the final decline of that achievement after more than 300 years.

The *Britannia* was built in the famous shipyard of John Brown, Clydebank, who had built great ships for many years and battleships and aircraft

The *Britannia* dressed overall alongside at Leith. (Copyright The Royal Yacht *Britannia*)

Bow view of the *Britannia* dressed overall at Leith. (Copyright The Royal Yacht *Britannia*)

carriers in the Second World War. She was built at the behest of King George VI, to replace the old Royal Yacht, *Victoria & Albert III*, which was very venerable and had herself served for half-a-century. An original feasibility study was done in 1938 and drawings made the following year, but the outbreak of war had put all such developments on hold until 1951 when a reduced scale design was discussed. A large number of fitments and furniture from the earlier vessel, many having associations with Prince Albert himself, were incorporated aboard the new ship including his famous gimbal table. Other historic features aboard included the ship's wheel of the racing yacht *Britannia* owned by King George V and the traditional binnacle on the veranda deck first embarked aboard the 1817 yacht, *Royal George*.

The *Britannia* was launched by Queen Elizabeth II on 16 April 1953, before an audience of 30,000 well-wishers just prior to her being crowned in June 1953, thus establishing a fond connection that lasted for half a century. The Queen herself had chosen the new ship's name. The *Britannia* became a much-loved vessel and during her forty-four years of cruising the world was well-known to people the length and breadth of the globe, from remote Pacific islands to major cities in every continent. The cost of *Britannia* was £2,098,000 and, to offset this figure, the official design was always that *Britannia* could be quickly converted into a hospital ship in the event of a major conflict, but this never, in fact, occurred, not even during the Falklands War in the 1980s. Certainly in 1954 the Admiralty conducted a series of tests which they stated proved that such an emergency conversion was perfectly feasible. Right from the onset, however, *Britannia* incorporated features deemed essential in a hospital ship role, such as Denny-Brown stabilizers, air-conditioning and vibration-free running, and these were retained when other facilities were scaled back on grounds of cost. A series of conversion options was prepared for such an eventuality, dependant upon time scales. A two-day conversion could accommodate 180 patients and appropriate medical supplies; a ten-day alteration increased this to 255 patients plus a dispensary, X-ray area and dental surgery. In such an eventuality the Royal Navy

crew would be replaced by a mercantile one but, in the event, the closest she came to this role was in the evacuation of British nationals trapped by civil unrest in South Yemen in January 1986.

The *Britannia* was first commissioned on 11 January 1954. She later carried the IMO 8635306 in service. *Britannia* was designed by Sir Victor Shepheard, Director of Naval Construction; she displaced 4,715 tons with a gross tonnage of 5,862 tons; and had an overall length of 125.65m (412ft 3in, with a waterline length of 115.82m (380ft) and length between perpendiculars of 109.73m (360ft). Her maximum moulded breadth was 16.76m (55ft) and mean draught was 5.2m (15ft 7in).

Her best speed, provided by her two geared high-pressure steam turbines, which developed 12shp, was 21.5 knots. These turbines had been designed by John Brown with the help of Parsons & Marine Engineering Research & Development Association (Pamatrada) when turbo-electric propulsion had been rejected. Her two propellers were of 3.12m (10ft 3 in) diameter. Her two main boilers, plus an auxiliary boiler for harbour work, were Foster Wheeler, and she had a 2,553 nautical mile range at 18 knots. She could originally carry

The ship's bell of HM Yacht *Britannia*. (Copyright The Royal Yacht *Britannia*)

Table set for dinner aboard HM Yacht *Britannia*. (Copyright The Royal Yacht *Britannia*)

330 tons of fuel oil and 120 tons of fresh water but additional tanks extended this bunkerage. The heights of her three masts from the ship's water-line were – foremast 40.54m (133ft); mainmast – 42.44m (13ft 3in) and mizzen 36.22m (118ft 10in) respectively. Three masts were always deemed essential for a Royal Yacht so that she could display simultaneously the Royal Standard (Main) the Lord High Admiral's flag (Fore) and the Union Flag (Mizzen).

The Royal Yacht was also designed from the beginning to act as a floating reception venue of the highest calibre. Aboard her were sumptuous state apartments with catering facilities for some 250 guests, as well as offices for the Royal House-hold. She had a cinema and a laundry. Other areas included Their Majesty's Sitting Rooms,

the dining-room, drawing-room and ante-room, household and guest cabins, sitting- and cloak-rooms fitted out to first-class liner standard. She originally carried the following service boats – a 12.192m (40ft) Royal Barge from the *Victoria and Albert*, which was used at the Coronation Review in June 1953; two 10.668m (35ft) motor boats, a 9.753 (32ft) motor cutter, two 8.229m (27ft) jolly boats, two 4.87m (16ft) fast motor dinghies and two 4.267m (14ft) sailing dinghies.

Her first voyage was to take the Queen home to London from Tobruk in Libya in 1954, sailing up the Thames to the Pool of London to disembark her. She made a stirring entrance with her single raking funnel, clipper bow and balanced upper-works, with Royal accommodation aft and crew accommodation forward.

The crew of the Royal Yacht, every man a volunteer, were known as Royal Yachtsmen and the standard was uniformly high. There were ultimately nineteen officers and 217 of the latter and Royal Marine Bands were embarked for special occasions. While the normal period of duty in such a demanding environment was a two-year stint, some men served aboard her for twenty years. There were never any navy defaulters reporting for punishment aboard the *Britannia*; any lapse from the required code of conduct immediately resulted in a return to the nearest warship or shore establishment with no appeal. The *Britannia* was also unique as a naval vessel in that no broadcasting system or ship's piping system to call hands to duties was ever installed aboard her nor were bugle calls permitted. Piping aboard was confined strictly to Her Majesty, or the Duke of Edinburgh should she not be present and he was in uniform. Silent efficiency was the order of the day at all times for her crew and each day's duties were posted up as Daily Orders to be read fully, digested and carried out without question. The crew wore gym shoes while aboard as part of this silent routine and spoken words of command were few and far between, efficiency being relied upon by hand signals in the main. There were two 3-pounder saluting guns fitted on the compass platform for the traditional morning and evening salutes when the Queen was embarked. When the Royal Barge was utilised by the Queen it was always under the command of the Commodore Royal Yachts or his representative.

Other customs related to privacy for the Royal Party, and the strictest rules were in place to prevent discussion on events. The area of the

Informal seating area with period decor aboard the Royal Yacht *Britannia*. (Copyright The Royal Yacht *Britannia*)

Britannia abaft the mainmast, when the Royal Standard was flying, was strictly enforced as part of this routine and the Captain's permission had to be obtained, other than for essential duties, for any officer or man to go into this area later than 0900. If a Yachtsman had to go to the quarter-deck on any vital mission there was a passage via the Engineer Officer's flat for such access that would not disturb the Royal guests, and caps were never worn in these instances. The uniform included the traditional black memorial band on the cap tallies in memory of Prince Albert originally incorporated at the behest of Queen Victoria. These special touches all made for a unique service period while aboard. Even her ship's engine rooms, by their nature not the easiest of areas to keep clean, were kept immaculate, being the only ship in the Royal Navy to have a mat at the entrance on which every crew member entering had to wipe his feet.

The end of that proud heritage was announced in June 1994, the Government stating that they could no longer afford such a ship. Although many leading British industrialists, who knew what a great promoter of trade she was, offered to stump up the cash, the then Chancellor apparently turned them down as well, no doubt for excellent political reasons. One reason put forward for her demise was that she was the only remaining Royal Navy ship operating on Furnace Fuel Oil (FFO) when the rest of the fleet had converted to kerosene and so she could not refuel at sea. The cost of re-equipping her with new boilers and power plant was deemed prohibitive.

The last official voyage that *Britannia* undertook was to Hong Kong, that colony itself being handed over to Communist China and symbolically marking the final termination of Britain's maritime greatness and what it had achieved. Her final voyage with the Queen embarked was a visit to the Isle of Arran on 9 August 1997. The final decommissioning ceremony took place, appropriately enough, at Portsmouth Naval Base from where most of her voyages had commenced and terminated and was attended by the Queen herself, who shed a tear in public, the Duke of Edinburgh and a dozen other members of the Royal Family who had so often trodden her decks. More than 2,000 former Royal Yacht officers and crew, along with their families, also attended her last paying off. The *Britannia* had sailed an incredible 1,750,359.55 kilometres (1,087,623 nautical miles) in her lifetime. It was expected that either London or Portsmouth would be her most logical final resting place but politics intervened and a competition was held, with Edinburgh being declared the winner. Her new owners became a charity, The Royal Yacht *Britannia* Trust, with the sole remit of preserving her for posterity and she was docked at Leith.

She now is one of Scotland's premier tourist attractions and is open to visitors and also has been adapted as a major hospitality venue for grand occasions. The most recent function was also, appropriately, one to which the Royal Family was once more welcomed aboard. This was the pre-marriage cocktail party held on 30 July 2011, prior to the wedding of the Queen's granddaughter, Zara Philips, to England rugby star Mike Tindell. Among those attending on board that night were the Duke and Duchess of Cambridge, the Duke and Duchess of Wessex, Prince Harry, Princess Beatrice and Princess Eugenie.

The Royal Yacht *Britannia* currently resides at Ocean Terminal, Leith, Edinburgh, EH6 6JJ. Tel: 0131-555-0556. The Royal Yacht *Britannia* Trust has its registered office at Princes Exchange, 1 Earl Grey Street, Edinburgh, EH3 9EE.

GLENLEE (THE TALL SHIP)

Launched on Thursday 3 December 1896 the steel-built, three-masted sailing vessel (SV) *Glenlee* was a barque built for Archibald Sterling & Co. Ltd, Glasgow by Archibald Rodger & Company at Bay Yard, Port Glasgow (Yard No. 325). This very fine vessel was one of the famed 'Cape Horners' that plied their basic mercantile trade under sail well into the twentieth century. She had a gross registered tonnage (GRT) of 2,757, (1,613 net registered tonnage or NRT) an overall length with the spike bowsprit mounted of 86m (282ft); with a length of 74.9m (245.65ft), a breadth of 11.9m (38.9ft) and a draught of 5.4m (17.7ft). Her sail plan included double top- and topgallants, but not royals, a rig termed 'Bald headed'. She was operated by Sterling Shipping Company, Glasgow.

On 13 December she sailed for Liverpool in ballast to embark a general cargo for Portland, Oregon beginning a trading career under sail that was to last for twenty-three years including the perils of the First World War. On 25 March 1898

The Tall Ship – the *Glenlee* moored alongside the Riverside Museum, Glasgow. (Copyright and Courtesy of The Tall Ship/ Tom Finnie)

she was sold to Robert Ferguson & Co. Ltd, Dundee and the following year she was re-named *Islamount*. On 6 August 1900 she grounded at Holyhead but without too much damage.

She arrived at Liverpool on 23 August 1905 having completed a bulk cargo voyage from London to Australia and back to Falmouth, where she had been acquired by Richard Thomas & Co. Ltd, Criccieth, north Wales, and later Liverpool, who headed up a group who managed her as the single-ship Flint Castle Ship Co. She was mooted to be re-named *Flint Castle* but this was never done. For the next eleven years to 1916 her Captain remained Richard Owens of Nefyn, north Wales. On 20 December 1909 she received an evaluation by C. W. Kellocks, the Liverpool shipbrokers, of between £4,750 and £4,800.

She escaped with another near miss in February 1917, when, under tow off Melbourne, her hawser parted and she almost grounded. During 1918, at the height of the U-boat scare, she was placed under the management of John Stewart & Co. Ltd, London on behalf of the British Shipping Controller until October 1919. Up to this point in her life under the Red Duster the gallant old vessel had circumnavigated the world four times and had rounded the feared Cape Horn on no fewer than fourteen different occasions.

In 1920 she was sold to Societa Di Navigazione 'Stella Di Italiana', Milan. She then underwent some modernisation at Genoa, which, in 1922, included being fitted with a pair of auxiliary diesel engines. In 1922 she was again renamed, becoming the *Clarastella* and, on 29 March 1922, she was bought by the Spanish Government as a sail training ship. She once more underwent extensive rebuilding at Cautieu Navale Triestino (Trieste), Italy, in order for her to accommodate a 307 complement of trainees, and was renamed as the *Galatea*. By 1927 she was listed as a training ship for non-commissioned officers. The Escuela Naval Militar de Oficiales (ENM), the Naval Officers' Training School, was originally established at San Carlos, near San Fernando, Cadiz and most Spanish naval officers were trained there. In 1943 the school moved to Marí, Pontevedra in north-west Spain. Modifications to the *Clarastella*

included the installation of a flying bridge on her poop deck to aid manoeuvring.

Her third lucky escape took place in October 1946, when she was caught in a violent storm and lost almost all her rigging. Somehow she staged through and sought safety in Santa Cruz de Tenerife. By 1968 she had ceased sail training and was reduced to a static rigged sail training vessel at El Ferrol del Caudillo. In 1981 she was dry-docked and had new plating emplaced beneath the waterline to keep her sound and afloat. The idea was to sail her as part of the celebrations of the Olympic Games at Seville. However, the Government abruptly cancelled all the funding for this. Instead, her rig was much reduced, with her spars cut up like firewood and unceremoniously piled up ashore. In this sorry state she was towed to Saville, with the intent of using her as a museum, but in fact she became virtually abandoned, totally uncared for or protected. Not surprisingly, gangs of hooligans boarded and looted her, taking any item of potential sale value they could find, among them her bronze sea-cock valve and she sank at her berth. The cost of salvage was high and the wreck was scheduled to be broken up.

Fortunately, in the nick of time, Dr Sir John Brown, a famous British naval architect, came upon her and returned home determined to ensure the safety of this unique Clyde-built vessel before it was too late. The Spanish Navy sold her by auction and, on 30 June 1992, she was sold to the Clyde Maritime Trust for £40,000. She was docked and the Spanish additions mainly stripped out of her, including the flying bridge, to make her seaworthy once more.

On 6 July 1993 she returned to the Clyde under tow from Spain and upon arrival the Lord Provost of Glasgow re-named her *Glenlee*. Restoration was commenced by The Clyde Maritime Trust to restore her to her original condition and preserve her as a museum ship at Yorkhill Quay, Glasgow. The *Glenlee* Ship Committee under Hamish Hardie was established and they sought out the few remaining skilled men who could undertake such work in an age where shipbuilding was sparse and rigging magnificent sailing vessels almost a totally lost art. Fortunately such men were found,

The impressive masts and rigging of The Tall Ship – the *Glenlee* moored at the Riverside Museum Glasgow.
(Copyright and Courtesy of The Tall Ship/Tom Finnie)

including an expert rigger who trained up a team which carried out the complex work between April and December 1998. In all, 548.64m (18,000ft) of wire of various sizes and 350.52m (11,500ft) of rope were employed on the job. Her original masts were re-stepped and yards re-crossed. Other essential work included the removal of propellers and the restoration of her original figurehead and deckhouses.

In July 1999 she was docked at Greenock and repainted in readiness for her showing at the Cutty Sark Tall Ships' Race that month, before being towed to her normal berth. Since August 1999 the *Glenlee* has been operational as a museum ship. There are four other tall ships built on the Clyde that have also survived, the *Balclutha, Falls of Clyde, Moshulu* and *Pommern*, the first three at various ports in the USA (San Francisco, Hawaii and Philadelphia), the latter in the Aland Islands.

She is now moored alongside the Clyde Maritime Centre at Pointhouse Quay, as part of the new Glasgow Transport Museum and marketed as a major Glasgow tourist attraction as *The Tall Ship*. Fully recognised by the National Historic Ships' Committee, the *Glenlee* lies alongside the Riverside Museum and hosts exhibitions, festivals and has a series of educational courses. The Tall Ship receives an annual grant from Glasgow City Council and is manned by both a paid crew and volunteers.

WAVERLEY

One of the best-loved and most appreciated of Britain's old-timers, the Paddle Steamer *Waverley* is still a very busy lady with full schedule of sailings all around the UK coast right through 2011. However, she is now in dire need of TLC to keep her going and back up the valuable Heritage Lottery Fund contributions that have meant so much in recent years.

The *Waverley* (IMO 5386954 and MMSA 232001540), named from Sir Walter Scott's Waverley novels, which he named after the Cistercian monastery Waverley Abbey in Surrey, has the call sign GRPM as a fully operational vessel. She is of 693 gross tonnage with a length of 73.13m (239ft 6in) a beam of 17.45m (57ft 3in) and a 1.9m (6ft 3in) draught. She was built on the River Clyde by A. & J. Inglis at Pointhouse, Glasgow, (Yard No.1330P). Her keel was laid on 27 December 1945, and she was launched by Lady Matthews, wife of the then Chairman of the LNER, on 2 October 1946. Her total building coast was £107,725, the Admiralty contributing £15,125

The *Waverley*, which still operates in various parts of the United Kingdom as a pleasure craft as she has done for decades. (Copyright & Courtesy Peter McCann)

as compensation for the loss of her forebear in action.

Originally built with a coal-fired double-ended Scotch boiler built by Rankin & Blackmore at the Eagle Foundry, Greenock, her diagonal triple-expansion steam engine (No. 520) was converted to oil-firing in 1956. The *Waverley* initially ran her official acceptance trials between 2 and 5 June and made her maiden voyage on 16 June 1947. She has 2,100ihp (1,566kW) power and she achieved a best speed of 18.37 knots on the sea trials in 1947, although nowadays this has become a 14-knot service speed as more befits an elderly, but still game, lady. She can carry a maximum of 925 passengers. To cater for them she has a grand dining saloon and two separate bars.

Waverley was originally built in 1947 for the ferry arm of the London and North Eastern Railway which served the Firth of Clyde and which, following the 1948 railway nationalisation, became the Caledonian Steam Packet Company. She was the replacement for the previous *Waverley* which was sunk at Dunkirk in 1940 and was built to serve the Craigendorran Pier, Helensburgh, ferry route up Loch Long to Arrochar in western Scotland. Despite this limited original agenda, almost seventy years on she still plies UK waters from Easter to the autumn, being a famous sight anywhere from the Thames to the Bristol Channel and all along the south coast of England as well as along the Clyde in the Irish Sea and off the Western Isles. She is truly a legend, as was her predecessor.

This earlier *Waverley*, also a paddle steamer built in 1899, was taken over at the outbreak of the Second World War by the Admiralty who

The port bow view of the *Waverley*, showing her wide bridge paddle box as she pulls away from her anchorage.
(Copyright & Courtesy Peter McCann)

converted her for minesweeping. But it was her exploits during the evacuation of the British Expeditionary Force from the Dunkirk beaches in the dark days of June 1940 that made her immortal. The *Waverley* was part of the 12th Minesweeping Flotilla, composed of old paddle steamers which normally worked out of Harwich. They arrived off the Dunkirk beaches at midnight on Wednesday 29 May 1940, *Waverley* being under the command of Lieutenant S. F. Harmer-Elliott RNVR. During the course of the day she embarked about 600 soldiers ferrying from the beaches in small boats until she was full to capacity and, at 1520, started for Dover. The Luftwaffe was everywhere relatively unopposed and she was attacked by a force of twelve Heinkel He111 twin-engined bombers dropping their bombs from 2,348.4m (8,000ft) in succession. Despite taking her best evasive action there were several near misses, one of which tore off her rudder leaving her helpless. Another bomber then attacked and scored a direct hit on her ward-room, the bomb passing on down through the ship's bottom. She soon filled with water and sank very quickly, with the loss of two-thirds of the troops and many of the crew although some, including the captain, were rescued by the auxiliary *Crested Eagle*.

The 'new' *Waverley* dutifully served her assigned ferry route for almost thirty years, during which time the various small and independent separate ferry companies were absorbed into David MacBrayne Ltd which, in 1973, was re-branded as Caledonian MacBrayne. It proved increasingly difficult down the years to make the ageing *Waverley* profitable on her route with her old technology and, in 1974, she was withdrawn from service with the hope expressed that she might at least be preserved. Fortunately the very active and enthusiastic 4,000-strong Paddle Steamer Preservation Society (PSPS) came to the rescue and purchased her for the nominal sum of £1.

As a result of a most successful appeal for public funds, the *Waverley* was gradually restored to her original service, including being re-boilered in 1981. With a complete restoration between 2000 and 2003 at the Great Yarmouth shipyard of George Prior, which also involved the fitting of another new boiler, the Babcock Steambloc, and bringing her electronics and technology up to twenty-first-century safety standards, she resumed operations as part of Waverley Excursions, a group that currently includes the PS *Kingswear Castle* with the mv *Balmoral* as support vessel, both also described in these pages, and the *Maid of the Loch* preserved as a static display on Loch Lomond.

The *Waverley* is now the last seagoing passenger-carrying paddle steamer still operating in the entire world, and that fact alone ought to ensure her continued employment and usage. Her on-board facilities and amenities include an art deco restaurant with seating for 100 guests on the main deck and there are two bars, Jeanie Deans, a lounge with a 200-person capacity and the Lower Bar, with a wide range of malt whiskies as well as real ales. In addition, there is the Caledonian Tea Room on the promenade deck with seating for sixty. The *Waverley* has an observation lounge with wonderful views on the same deck seating twenty-five passengers.

A group of dedicated volunteers continually work to keep her in prime condition. Meanwhile the Paddle Steamer Preservation Society, with branches in London and the Home Counties, Bristol, Wessex, Scotland and in the North of England and Wales, is constantly carrying out improvements and running special excursions. Enquiries can be made to Waverley Excursions, 36 Lancefield Quay, Glasgow, G3 8HA or telephone 0845-130 4647

BRONINGTON

This little vessel was one of the Coniston or Ton-class coastal minesweepers built between 1951 and 1959. This class had a displacement of 440 tons, a length of 46.634m (153ft), a beam of 8.808m (28.9ft) and a draught of 2.499m (8.2ft). They were armed with one single-barrelled 40mm/L60 Bofors gun forward and had a complement of five officers and thirty-one ratings. These coastal minesweepers, of which the Royal Navy built 116, were among the most numerous classes of ships to have been built for the Royal Navy which, at that time, was obsessed with Soviet minelaying potential and built many coastal and inshore ships to cope with the perceived threat. Wooden-hulled to give immunity to magnetic mines, her hull was built of mahogany with a combination of aluminium alloys, making them the last conventional minesweepers and the last of the 'wooden walls' of Royal Navy tradition.

The earlier ships of this class with built with open bridges and lattice masts but the later builds had enclosed bridges and tripod masts and the older ships converted to this layout to comply with the NBC[3] concept of running the ships completely closed off from the outside world.

The *Bronington* (M1115), named from a village near Wrexham, was originally fitted with Mirrlees engines but these were later replaced with the lighter twin Napier Deltic 18A-7A 2,200kW (3,000hp) diesel engines. They gave her an operational range of 3,701.49km (2,300 miles).

Her maximum speed was 16 knots, running on both engines, or 13 knots running on just one. Their minimum speed was 6 knots which made manoeuvring into small harbours very difficult.

The *Bronington* was built by Cook Welton & Gemmel at Hull and Beverley, being laid down on Wednesday 30 May 1951 and launched on Thursday 19 March 1953 by Mrs W. G. John, wife of the Director, Naval Constructors. She was completed for service on Friday 4 June 1954 and was renamed as HMS *Humber* for service with the Humber Division of the Royal Naval Reserve until it was disbanded in 1958. During her time here the *Bronington* was awarded the Thornycroft Trophy for minesweeping excellence, beating both regular Navy and Reserve ships. She served with the 10th Minesweeper Squadron (MSS) RNR. In 1958 she re-assumed her name as HMS *Bronington* and joined the 100th MMS. She was later converted to a minehunter in 1965 at Rosyth Dockyard. Her open bridge was enclosed, the lattice mast replaced by a tripod and the newest mark of sonar fitted. Thus updated, in February 1965, she recommissioned in the 5th MMS at HMS *Vernon*, Portsmouth, before she was assigned to the 1st MCMS (Mine Counter-Measures Squadron) at Port Edgar. Here her role changed to mine counter-measures vessel, in that she used her high-definition sonar gear to locate mines which, once pinpointed, were then nullified by using clearance divers with explosive charges, or defused inboard. She could use her towed acoustic and magnetic influence sweeps, which imitated the profile of larger vessels and detonated them at a distance. She underwent a major refit at Gibraltar in 1974 and on completion again served with the 1st MCMS at Rosyth. Between 9 February and 15 December 1976 her commanding officer was HRH Lieutenant The Prince of Wales, during

---

3. The NBC (Nuclear, Biological and Chemical) concept involved the isolation of essential areas of the ship into sealed citadels to prevent contamination of vital areas in case of attacks by the above type weapons from any hostile force, either combat or terrorist.

The minesweeper HMS *Bronington*, a former command of HRH Prince Charles, in Gilrook Basin, Birkenhead, listing and awaiting her fate. (Copyright and Courtesy of Mark Hyland)

which time she visited the Pool and London and was visited by Her Majesty Queen Elizabeth II, HRH The Queen Mother, HRH Prince Philip and eight other members of the Royal Family. Between 1980 and 1984 she was with the 2nd MCMS and then served in the Mediterranean before returning home as part of NATO's STANAVFORCHAN (Standing Naval Force Channel) and on fishery protection duties.

The *Bronington* was decommissioned at Portsmouth on 23 June 1988 when she was taken over by the *Bronington* Trust, with Prince Charles as its Patron, and, from 28 October 1992, was moored at Salford Quays in the Manchester Ship Canal. In 2002 she was handed over to the Warship Preservation Trust and, on 11 July, dressed overall, tugs shifted her berth and towed her down to Birkenhead at a cost of £5,000 where for a time she was open to the public. She joined a

flotilla which contained the frigate *Plymouth*, submarine *Onyx*, *Landfall* (*LCT 7074*) and a German U-boat, *U-534*. When the Trust went into voluntary liquidation, these ships were closed to visitors on 5 February 2006 and taken over by the Mersey Docks and Harbour Company. The *Bronington* was later moved to the Vittoria Dock, close by the equally derelict frigate HMS *Plymouth* where they were left to rot. The *LCT 7074* sank at her moorings, the *U-534* was sold to a Danish consortium while the *Onyx* was purchased and moved to Barrow.

The *Bronington* is, at the time of writing, located in the Gillrook Basin (West Float) at Birkenhead in a very poor condition. Although still listed as part of the National Historic Fleet, her fuel tanks are removed and she was converted to incorporate a function room aft. Her deck has rotted and is in dire need of replacement as it leaks and this has ruined many fixtures and fittings below. At the time of writing, Philip Sommerville had expressed hopes to save her, but, depending on her condition, thought he might have to dismantle her if she is too far gone. The same person also stated that he intended to purchase a sister ship, HMAS *Curlew* (the former HMS *Cheddiston*) and sail her back to the United Kingdom for preservation, possibly incorporating parts of the *Bronington*. His intention was to relay the decks with treated marine ply covered with Sikaflex, replace her generators and fuel tanks and bulkheads, add S and X band radar, auto pilot, sonar set and alter her bridge. A possible berth for these vessels, if saved, was said to be at Shoreham, Sussex and for her to be used by sea cadets. However, attempts by various parties, other than Mr Sommerville, to agree details with Mersey Docks and Harbour Board have not progressed at all at the time of writing and, by the time this book is published, she may no longer exist.

PLYMOUTH

HMS *Plymouth* (F-126) was a Type 12, Rothesay-class frigate built for the Royal Navy by Devonport Dockyard, Plymouth. She was laid down on 1 July 1958, launched on 20 July 1959 by the Right Honourable Nancy, Viscountess Astor CH, and commissioned on 11 May 1961. She was the ninth ship to carry this name in the service of the Royal Navy.

The first warship so named was a Commonwealth Navy Speaker-class frigate, initially equipped with fifty-two guns and built at Wapping by Taylour in 1653. She had an overall length of 35.4m (116ft), a beam of 10.6m (34ft 8in) and a tonnage 753. She was named at the time in honour of the stern defence of the town of Plymouth during the English Civil War. She served at the battles of Porto Farina in 1655, Santa Cruz in 1657, and Lowestoft in 1665, at the Four Days' Battle in 1666, at Orfordness the same year, at Solebay in 1672, and at the Texel in 1673. She was re-armed in 1677 to carry sixty guns and was at the Battle of Bantry Bay in 1689. Her final battle was at Beachy Head in 1690. Following more than half a century of superb service she was taken in hand and rebuilt in 1705, her new dimensions being a gun-deck length of 42.8m (140ft 5in), a beam of 11.7m (38ft 3in) and a tonnage of 911.4 as a fourth-rate ship-of-the-line but she foundered in a storm almost immediately. Another *Plymouth* had been a sheer hulk used to hoist masts out of serving ships, which was bought in 1689, and she survived until 1730 before being broken up.

On 25 May 1708 a new sixty-gun fourth-rate was launched at Plymouth Dockyard to replace the first *Plymouth*. After some years' service she was taken apart and successfully rebuilt at Chatham Dockyard, being re-launched on 2 August 1722 and she survived until 1764 before being broken up. The prize ship *Plymouth* was a sixth-rate,

taken in 1709 but surrendered the same year. Meanwhile a six-gun brig, launched in 1755, had been in service and she served until 1793. A transport launched in 1778 was named *Plymouth* at this time and remained in use until 1815 when she was sunk as a breakwater. Similarly an eight-gun transport was launched as *Plymouth* in 1796 and not broken up until 1830, the same year as the former yacht *Admiralty* was renamed *Plymouth* for harbour duties. She was renamed *YC 1* in 1866, surviving for another four years until being sold out of service. The name then remained in abeyance, strangely enough, until the 1950s.

The frigate *Plymouth* was primarily designed as an anti-submarine vessel, and had an overall length of 112.78m (369.77ft), a draught of 5.18m (16.98ft) and a beam of 12.50m (40.98ft), with a standard displacement of 2,150 tons, and full load displacement tonnage of 2,560. Her armament was a twin Mark 6 11.43cm (4.5-inch) gun turret forward, a single Mark 7 40mm Bofors gun aft, and two Mark 10 Limbo anti-submarine mortars. Designed plans for twelve 53.34cm (21-inch) anti-submarine torpedo tubes never seem to have been installed, due, no doubt, to cost.

She had a crew of 152 as built, which was later increased to 225 and, with later modifications, to 235 which made her very cramped. She was equipped with Type 293Q target indication radar, Type 277Q height-finding radar, Type 275 fire-control radar on a Mark 6M Director and a Type 974 navigation radar. She also shipped the Type Mark 10 1010 Cossor IFF (Identification Friend or Foe), a Type 174 search sonar, a Type 162 target classification sonar and a Type 170 attack sonar as completed. The *Plymouth* was powered by two Babcock and Wilcox boilers with two English Electric steam turbines driving two shafts with 30,000shp giving her 30 knots top

HMS *Plymouth* at Vittoria Dock, Birkenhead, in an uncared-for state, rust-streaked and neglected. It is hoped that a more caring environment is found for her before it is too late. (Copyright and Courtesy of Mark Hyland)

speed. She could embark 400 tons of oil fuel, giving her an economical range of 9,600km (5,200 nautical miles) at 12 knots speed.

Her first assignment was to the 4th Frigate Squadron and subsequently to the 22nd and the 29th Escort Squadrons in the Far East where she participated in several exercises. Between 1966 and January 1969 *Plymouth* was modernised at Chatham Dockyard and her new armament included two 20mm guns, a Sea Cat GWS-20 surface-to-air missile (SAM) system, a Mk 10 mortar and a Westland Wasp (helicopter anti-submarine) HAS.1 as a medium-range anti-submarine torpedo carrying helicopter (MATCH) and she also had two 8-barrel 7.62cm (3-inch) Knebworth/Corvus countermeasures launchers fitted. Her electronics were also updated and she then carried a Type 993 target indication radar, a Type 903 fire control radar on a MRS3 director, a Type 978 navigation radar, a Type 1010 Cossor Mark 10 IFF while her three sonar outfits were a Type 177 search, a Type 162 target classification and a Type 170 attack set.

The *Plymouth* served worldwide during her service career, returning to the Indian Ocean, Far East, Australia and then back to Europe. She was again refitted at Devonport Dockyard before re-commissioning for the West Indies' Station, returning to home waters in February 1973 and

taking part in the so-called 'Cod War', as a fishing dispute with Iceland was termed by the media. She then went out to the Mediterranean before being docked at Gibraltar and subsequently returned to the UK on 11 December 1974.

This done, she joined the 8th Frigate Squadron and served in the Mediterranean, South China Sea and visited Australia, before sailing home via the United States, the Panama Canal and the Caribbean once more. She spent the next years in home waters, and was present at the Silver Jubilee Fleet Review at Spithead; she also served in the Mediterranean and the North Atlantic. Another refit followed between July 1978 and 23 January 1981.

In 1982 the *Plymouth* was in the forefront of a real war as part of the Royal Navy Task Force sent to free the Falklands Islands and South Georgia from the invasion and occupation forces of the Argentine Military Junta in 1982.

The *Plymouth*, along with the *Antrim* and the RFA *Tidepool*, sailed to the South Atlantic and joined the frigate *Brilliant* and ice patrol ship *Endurance* in the vanguard of the fleet that liberated South Georgia during Operation PARAQUAT on 28 April. A Royal Marine force was landed with *Plymouth* using her Westland Wasp helicopter to carry them ashore, and she conducted a bombardment with her twin 11.43cm (4.5-inch)

Port side broadside view of the frigate HMS *Plymouth*. (Copyright & Courtesy of Mike Thomas)

guns on the dug-in enemy forces on the island. The *Plymouth*'s Wasp also joined in a joint attack on the Argentine submarine *Santa Fe* which crippled her; her grounded hulk was captured by the Royal Marines as one of the first enemy casualties of the war.

Further bombardments were carried out in conjunction with the main fleet when the Falklands themselves were freed. The *Plymouth* was the first ship to enter the restricted San Carlos Water which proved a death trap. She stood by the frigate *Argonaut* which had been badly damaged by Argentine fighter-bombers. Then, during repeated Argentine air attacks on the fleet on 8 June, five of the FAA 6° Gruppo's Israeli-supplied Dagger fighter-bombers concentrated on *Plymouth* and, when her Sea Cat missiles failed to score any hits to deter them, got through her defences. The *Plymouth* was hit by four bombs and many cannon shells and badly damaged. A bomb struck her flightdeck, igniting her depth charges and starting a large fire; another perforated the ship's funnel while the other two wiped out her anti-submarine Limbo mortar. What saved the ship was the fact that the bombs had been dropped from too low a level and the fuses failed to detonate, or else she would have been lost. As it was these 'duds' injured just five of her crew, a lucky let-off. She was assisted in fighting the fires by the frigate *Avenger*. She was able to effect temporary repairs alongside the *Stena Seaspread* and was back in action again providing bombardment fire support and was the first warship to re-enter Port Stanley Harbour. It was aboard the *Plymouth*, in the ship's wardroom, that the surrender of the Argentine Forces in South Georgia was signed by Lieutenant Alfredo Astiz on 25 April. *Plymouth*'s record in the Falklands campaign was impressive; she had steamed 54,717.69km (34,000 miles), fired off more than 900 of her 11.43cm (4.5-inch) shells and claimed the destruction of several enemy aircraft.

The *Plymouth* then returned to the United Kingdom in company with the damaged destroyer *Glamorgan* on 21 June arriving at Rosyth on 14 July under her own power. At Rosyth Dockyard the *Plymouth* underwent a major refit and, in 1983, took her place as guardship on the West Indies'

Station, including protection work off the coast of Belize which was under threat from Guatemala. More damage was done on 11 March 1984, when the German frigate FGS *Braunschweig* collided with her, while, in 1986 a serious fire broke out in the ship's boiler room during which two of her crew died. She was repaired at Rosyth and went back to the Caribbean for the last time before returning home. She was by this time the last of the Type 12 frigates still serving and her time had clearly come. The *Plymouth* was decommissioned from the Royal Navy on 28 April 1988 after twenty-seven years' service.

Destined to be sunk as a target or sold to shipbreakers, the *Plymouth* was saved from those alternative fates by a team of volunteers with the backing of former Devonport MP, Dr David Owen, who wanted to preserve her for the nation. The MoD permitted her to be opened to the public at Trinity Pier, Millbay Docks, Plymouth as a one-year experiment. Although the Plymouth response was not totally successful, The Warship Preservation Trust stepped in and she was given a spruce-up at the Cammell Laird Shipyard and then moored at the East Float Dock, Birkenhead. The Wirral Borough Council assisted in keeping her open as a tourist attraction from May 1992 but by 2006 the Trust had gone into liquidation and, from 5 February, visitors were barred. Ideas for her to return to Plymouth, although receiving some public support, have been rejected by the City Council there with the words 'In the current economic climate it is imperative that there is no risk of these liabilities failing on the public purse'. Despite newspaper stories, Portsmouth also seemed to be lukewarm. So the *Plymouth*, which had not been seen as a liability during the liberation of the Falklands, appears doomed.

She is currently laid up in poor condition at the Vittoria Dock, Birkenhead and is no longer used as a floating museum. In July 2012 what was termed the 'Last Chance' to save the *Plymouth* from the firm of Turkish shipbreakers to which she had been sold was launched. It was hoped to raise £400,000 to terminate the contract to sell her and to sail her to an unspecified north-eastern port for preservation by the HMS *Plymouth* Trust.

CAROLINE

The light cruiser of the twentieth-century Royal Navy was the descendant of the fast frigate, as typified by the *Foudroyant*, of the nineteenth century and earlier. Her duties were the same, to scout ahead of the main battle fleet and locate and bring news of the strength and dispositions of the enemy ships. She had also to prevent the opposing fleet's scouting forces doing the same.

The first ship to be named *Caroline* in the service of the Royal Navy was a fifth-rate launched in 1795. She was so-named after the wife of George III's eldest son (later George IV). The ship's badge of the present *Caroline* depicts this connection, showing as it does a golden sceptre between a crowned rose and thistle. The sceptre is from the Arms of Brandenberg. The ship's motto is *Tenax propositi* which means 'firm of purpose'.

Five ships carried this name between 1795 and 1882 and so the present *Caroline* bears an honoured name in naval history. She was the name ship of a whole class of light cruisers laid down in the years preceding the Great War.

The original ship's nameplate aboard HMS *Caroline*
(Copyright and Courtesy of National Museum of the Royal Navy)

There were six ships of this class in total, the *Caroline* herself being built by the shipbuilding firm of Cammell Laird in the outstanding time of eleven months from the launching of her keel to her completion. This haste was due to the outbreak of the Great War in 1914 when all naval work was hurried forward in order to get the ships to sea.

The *Caroline* and her sisters were relatively small in comparison to contemporary types of cruisers in service at that time; she was launched at Birkenhead on 28 January 1914, and was commissioned on 4 December the same year. She displaced 3,750-tons and had a length of 135.94m (446ft) and a beam of 12.649m (41.5ft); she was armed with two 15.2cm (6-inch) guns, seven 10.2cm (4-inch) guns and one 7.62cm (3-inch) gun and carried four 53.34cm (21-inch) torpedo tubes in two twin mounts. The 10.2cm (4-inch) guns were later replaced by four more 15.2cm (6-inch) weapons. She was capable of a speed of 29 knots from her oil-fired boilers which drove her geared steam turbines, developing 40,000 shp for her four propellers. She had a complement of 325 officers and men. Despite her smallness, she and her sisters proved to be splendid ships in service and the design of the *Caroline* was utilised throughout the Great War as the basis for several further classes of light cruiser, some of which survived to serve again in the Second World War as anti-aircraft ships.

On completion the *Caroline* joined the Grand Fleet and, under the command of Captain Crooke, she was present at the Battle of Jutland. She was with the 4th Light Cruiser Squadron under Commodore Le Meurier, and, following the inconclusive main clash between the Battle Fleets, she was stationed abreast the 2nd Battle Squadron

HMS *Caroline* looking aft along her foredeck from the bows. (Copyright and Courtesy of National Museum of the Royal Navy)

during the night dispositions ordered by Admiral Jellicoe, the British Commander-in-Chief.

Here they sighted three German battleships at dusk over to the westward and turned to investigate further. They were soon able to confirm that the massive shapes glimpsed through the murk were indeed the enemy and informed Admiral Jerram of the 2nd Battle Squadron accordingly. They then steered very bravely to carry out their own attack on the German giants. Here was a chance to inflict further damage on the already badly battered High Seas Fleet whose only aim at this time was to reach the safety of their own ports. To do this they had to cross the British line of route, whereas it was Jellicoe's intention to keep between the Germans and their base and finish them off in the morning.

Unfortunately, Admiral Jerram was not convinced that what *Caroline* and her sisters had sighted were the Germans. He had fears that they might be the British battle-cruisers and he therefore took no action with his ships and signalled to *Caroline* and her consorts to attack only if quite sure. They were indeed quite sure and launched their torpedoes in the face of heavy fire. They were unlucky not to have scored any hits, for one of their torpedoes passed beneath a German battleship. However, the enemy then turned away and contact was lost and never again regained by the main British fleet. War is full of 'might-have-beens' but it is interesting to speculate on what the outcome of the battle would have been had the battleships followed *Caroline* towards the Germans.

Looking along the planked foredeck of HMS *Caroline* towards her bows. (Copyright and Courtesy of National Museum of the Royal Navy)

The *Caroline* herself survived the war and continued to serve with the fleet until April 1924, when she was refitted and taken to Belfast to become the Royal Naval Volunteer Reserve drill ship at that port.

She performed this duty for many years and remained in good condition. During the Second World War she became the base ship at Belfast and was berthed at Alexandra Wharf as the Ulster Division's base ship for 130 reservists. It

HMS *Caroline's* funnels and bridge looking forward port side amidships.
(Copyright and Courtesy of National Museum of the Royal Navy)

was always hoped that, when her usefulness in this role finally came to a close, the Maritime Trust would preserve her as an example of the only Jutland warship still afloat today. The original plan was for move her to a berth near the *Warrior* as a museum ship although there are other plans to keep her at Belfast. Whatever her future location constitutes a link between the already secure *Foudroyant* and the later generation preserved light cruiser *Belfast* in our naval history.

HMS *Caroline*, showing the port bridge wing supports. (Copyright and Courtesy of National Museum of the Royal Navy)

TRINCOMALEE

This gallant old lady is the second oldest warship still afloat and as such is worth of special attention. She was ordered for the Royal Navy on 30 October 1812, and was laid down at the East India Company Dockyard at Bombay (Mumbai) Dockyard on 25 April 1814 under the direction of Jamsetjee Bomanjee Wadia, the Master Builder at that time.

Both she and her sister ship, the *Amphitrite*, were built from the plans of the thirty-six-gun frigates of the Leda class built at Chatham Dockyard, but the *Trincomalee* as she was named in honour of the naval encounter with the French off Ceylon (Sri Lanka as it is currently called) in 1782 were somewhat altered. The function of the frigate in the eighteenth and nineteenth century navy corresponded to that of the light cruiser in the twentieth century, scouting ahead of the main fleet. While the great ships of the line, as typified by the *Victory*, fought the major actions, it was the faster, lightly-armed frigates that searched ahead of the main squadrons to bring news of the enemy but, of course, they were always eager to bring to action the frigates of the enemy fleet. Thus many of the Navy's most famed and gallant single-ship actions were those fought by the frigates.

The *Trincomalee* was launched on 12 October 1817 and had a waterline length of 47.5m (156ft) and an overall length of 54.864m (180ft), with a beam of 12.344m (40.5ft). Her tonnage was 1,066 and displacement 1,447 tons. She was constructed as a sailing frigate and had a sail area of 1,692.95m^2 (17,254ft^2), excluding stuffing sails, staysails, royals and flying jib. These gave her a speed of around 14 knots.

She differed from similar frigates built in home waters in that her hull and fittings were constructed from Malabar teak, whereas her contemporaries were of traditional oak. Teak-built ships proved to be stronger vessels but oak construction was preferred by the seamen because whereas a splinter wound from an oaken ship stayed clean that from a teak ship festered.

The *Trincomalee* was launched in 1817 on 12 October, some two years since the end of the Napoleonic wars, and this, plus her sturdy construction, did much to ensure her long life both in and out of the service. She was three-masted and was rated as a fifth rate. She carried forty-four guns as designed and had a crew of twenty-four officers, thirty-nine petty officers, 115 seamen, thirty-three boys and twenty-nine Royal Marines.

In fact *Trincomalee* was not commissioned when first completed, due to the end of hostilities, and, in 1835, she was much altered to follow the plan of Sir William Symonds, Surveyor of the Navy. An elliptical stern was substituted for the original which gave a much wider arc to the 20.3cm (8-inch) stern gun and the two after guns on the main deck. She was still in reserve in 1845 and, on being examined, the hull of the twenty-eight-year old vessel was found to be in excellent condition, despite this enforced idleness. She was therefore taken in hand for further modernisation, again on the lines of Sir William Symonds' designs, to conform to the all big-gun concept of a frigate.

She was subsequently re-rated as a twenty-six-gun vessel in 1845 when she was armed with two 25.4cm (10-inch), two 20.3cm (8-inch) and twenty-two 32-pounder guns. In this condition her displacement was reduced to 1,215 tons. She commissioned for the first time for a three-year period on the North American and West Indies' Station under the command of Captain Richard Laird Warren RN on 23 July 1847. The commission ended in August 1850.

In 1851 the *Trincomalee* was further re-rated to a twenty-four-gun frigate when she was re-

The frigate *Trincomalee* in dock at Hartlepool. (Copyright and Courtesy of Dr Phil Brown – www.docbrown.info/docspics)

armed with ten 20.3cm (8-inch), eight 24-pounder, four 32-pounder and two 56-pounder guns, all muzzle-loaders. She was then re-commissioned at Plymouth in July 1852 under the command of Captain Wallace Houstoun RN for service with the Pacific Squadron. Here she spent an eventful five years calling at Rio before rounding the Horn and spending her time between the Falkland Islands and the Aleutians, Tahiti and Petropavlovsk. During the period of the Crimean War she cruised in Russian waters, on 25 June exchanging three Russian prisoners of war for a British and a French seaman at Avacha Bay, Kamchatka. She did not return again to Plymouth until September 1857, being laid up 'in ordinary'.

With the coming of the ironclads, as described in our section on the *Warrior*, the *Trincomalee's* days with the active fleet were finally over but, between 1860 and 1890, she was gainfully employed as the Royal Naval Reserve Drill Ship at Sunderland, being tender to the *Castor* and, in 1862, to the Union Dock at Hartlepool, under Captain Thomas Head RN. During this long period she was visited by Gladstone in his capacity of Honourable Elder Brother of Trinity House. Between 1870 and 1873 the *Trincomalee* was extensively refitted for her training role and, four years later, taken south once more to Southampton Water, still as a drill ship receiving yet further alterations in 1877 and again in 1881.

By the early 1890s, she was replaced by HMS *Medea* and destined for the lowly role of depot ship but was, instead, sold to the Portsmouth shipbreakers' yard of Reed's. She was saved from this melancholy fate in 1897 by the intervention of Mr G. Wheatley Cobb who purchased the *Trincomalee* in 1898 to replace Nelson's old

frigate *Foudroyant*, which had been wrecked off Blackpool. Between 1897 and 1902 she underwent a large rebuilding at Cowes, Isle of Wight, to prepare her and was repainted at Falmouth. In 1903 the *Trincomalee* was accordingly renamed as the Training Ship (TS) *Foudroyant* in honour of that vessel which was so much loved by the little Admiral when in the Mediterranean and, under this new name, she was utilised as a training ship; in 1927 she was transferred to a new base at Milford Haven.

When Mr Cobb died, to secure her future the TS *Foudroyant* was presented to the Society of Nautical Research in 1932 and they utilised her in conjunction with the *Implacable* at Portsmouth, being administered by the *Implacable* Committee, but she remained a youth training ship between

The guns on the quarterdeck of the frigate *Trincomalee*. (Copyright and Courtesy of Dr Phil Brown – www.docbrown.info/docspics)

the wars. During the period 1941–47, the old ship re-entered naval service when both vessels were commandeered by the Admiralty at Portsmouth as naval store ships, the pair being administered as a single unit when the new aircraft carrier *Implacable* joined the fleet to prevent confusion, and jointly known as HMS *Foudroyant* from 1943. Former sea cadets, who joined the Royal Navy as Hostilities Only ratings (known as Bounty Boys) received initial training aboard her until the war was over.

In 1949 the old *Implacable* was scuttled at sea as she had become unseaworthy, but fortunately a *Foudroyant* Committee prevented the same fate for her former companion and she carried on for another decade. In 1959 she was transferred to the *Foudroyant* Trust, with the declared intention of continuing the afloat training in Portsmouth harbour for as long as the old vessel was in a good enough condition for this to be done safely. The thought was that, when she finally could no longer be so employed, she would be preserved and that training could continue aboard her in a new berth.

Lord Montagu, then a Governor of the Trust, offered the ideal berth for the *Foudroyant*, at Buckler's Hard in Hampshire. Here, on the beautiful Beaulieu river, she could lie close by the famous Maritime Museum and the yard where so many of her contemporaries had been constructed, and form a central showpiece of a collection of ships and boats from those times.

The Maritime Trust also assisted in framing her future plans and, during 1972, the *Foudroyant* was dry-docked by Harland and Wolff at their number 5 dry-dock at Southampton. This duly took place between February and March, the last time she had been so examined having been at Pembroke Dock in 1905. A further docking followed to recaulk her decks and these dockings caused the shipwrights some headaches. Her unusual shape below the waterline meant that she could not be chocked up in the modern manner which meant bracing ten shores along each side. The trimming and bending of the replacement planks and frames was another job which a modern yard was not really equipped to handle. Fortunately, the results of the initial survey were to

find that in fact the *Foudroyant*'s condition underwater was much better than had at first been feared, her copper sheathing was still in good order, and the one soft spot was duly replaced.

The training as then given by the *Foudroyant* was in the arts of basic navigation, sailing and seamanship. The then schooling season extended from May to September and the various parties spent one to two week courses on the ship during which time, other than the cooking, they fended for themselves as much as possible. The majority of these parties were organised by schools and the teachers accompanied the children throughout the courses. They messed together, learnt to sling hammocks in the old tradition and day trips were organised to surrounding areas of interest and beauty, which made for a complete and very educationally rich course of self-reliance. The *Foudroyant*'s crew consisted of a captain, four or five specialist instructors, many of them being ex-naval men in those days, and some deckhands. There was a resident cook and nursing staff aboard during the season.

Both the Maritime Trust and the Society for Nautical Research expressed keen interest in her ultimate preservation and restoration and, when her hull was pronounced to be as strong and seaworthy as ever, there was hope that the *Foudroyant* would continue to provide this worthwhile service for many years. Being so used for many decades thus, the *Foudroyant*'s days as a training ship finally terminated in 1986 and she was then moved to Falmouth where she became a holiday ship and, following a short while there, was transferred to Portsmouth once more.

In July 1987 the *Trincomalee* was loaded aboard a barge and taken north, the move being funded by the Trust which saw Hartlepool as a safe haven for her, where she had resided over 100 years earlier. Five million pounds was estimated to be necessary to restore her to a mixture of both her 1817 and her 1847 state and exhibit her in a termagant dry-dock and join the old paddle steamer *Wingfield Castle*. She thus became one of the principal ships of the National Historic Fleet Core Collections and the major part of the Hartlepool 'Maritime Experience'. A continuing restoration programme followed from 1990 and lasted eleven years. Much of the accumulated additions and alterations were stripped from her, along with eighty tons of iron ballast and 140 of her 144 frames had to be replaced, using the cheaper Opepe wood rather than the original Malabar teak. Her original masting was replaced by steel look-alikes and she was re-coppered, while between decks replica cannon and artefacts

Detail including gun, shroud block and cat's head aboard the frigate *Trincomalee*. (Copyright and Courtesy of Dr Phil Brown – www.docbrown.info/ docspics)

were introduced, but, unlike most of her contemporaries, she remains 65 per cent original.

In April 1992 she reverted to her original name of *Trincomalee* and the HMS *Trincomalee*

Trust was established under the patronage of HRH The Duke of Edinburgh. She is berthed in the Graving Dock as the centrepiece of the exhibit.

The imposing ship's figurehead of the frigate *Trincomalee* at Hartlepool.
(Copyright and Courtesy of Dr Phil Brown – www.docbrown.info/docspics)

ONYX

This attack/patrol submarine was of the twenty-seven strong Oberon class, and a sister ship to the *Ocelot*, also described in this book. Originally ordered for the Royal Canadian Navy, *Onyx* (S21) belonged to the second, improved, group of this class and was one of the last to be built. She was laid down on 16 November 1964 but, while still under construction at Cammell Laird, Birkenhead, she was transferred to the Royal Navy and was launched in August 1966 and first commissioned in September 1967. Like her sisters, the *Onyx* was built of glass-fibre and alloy, the only such British submarine class to utilise these materials. She was of 1,610 tons standard, 2,030 tons surfaced displacement, and 2,410-tons submerged displacement, with an overall length of 88.5m (295ft 25in), 73.456m (241ft) between parallels, a beam of 8.1m (26.5ft) and a 5.5m (18ft) draught. She was powered by two Admiralty Standard Range 1, supercharged 16VMS – ASR1 diesel and two electric engines developing 3,680hp each, driving two shafts which gave her a high submerged speed of 17 knots and a surface speed of just 12 knots. She had a range of 19,170km (10,350 nautical miles) and could dive to a depth of 200m (650ft).

The *Onyx* was armed with eight 533.4m (21-inch) torpedo-tubes, six in the bow for Mark 24 wire-guided *Tigerfish* attack homing torpedoes and Mark 8 torpedoes, a design dating back to 1928 with an improved warhead from 1943; plus two short tubes as anti-submarine defence weapons in the stern. An alternative payload was up to fifty mines. She also carried Type 1002 surface search and navigation radar, a Type 187 active-passive attack sonar set and a Type 2007 long-range passive sonar set plus MEL Manta UAL or UA4 radar warning outfits and decoys. She later deployed the submarine version of the Harpoon guided weapon. Her complement was seven officers and sixty-two men.

The first official duty the *Onyx* performed was in July, as part of the 3rd Submarine Squadron based at Faslane in the Clyde, when she was put on display at Swansea Docks during the investiture of Prince Charles as The Prince of Wales and this was followed by visits to several other European ports. Her first visit to Portsmouth took place in October 1971, where she underwent a two-year refit. In 1973 her second commission was with the 1st Submarine Squadron, based at Gosport, during which period her acknowledged duties included spells in northern and home waters and the Mediterranean. In 1976 the *Onyx* was one of the Royal Navy ships sent to attend the United States Bicentennial Naval Review. A second refit at Portsmouth Dockyard followed and she re-commissioned for the third time, again with the 1st SS (Submarine Squadron), again in the Mediterranean and European waters. She had been participating in a training exercise off Portland and was visiting Plymouth, when the unprovoked Argentine invasion of the Falkland Islands occurred. She was promptly recalled to Gosport for orders.

On 26 April 1982 the *Onyx* became the only conventionally-powered submarine to be despatched to the South Atlantic for combat duties during the Falklands War during which she greatly distinguished herself conducting 'special operations', of which little or nothing was announced at the time. She was not fully combat-ready when despatched, however; there was a hole in one external fuel tank which leaked and gave her position away during the journey south. On reaching the staging post of Ascension Island, her Executive Officer went over the side and carried out the necessary repair at considerable

The submarine *Onyx* alongside HMS *Plymouth* at Liverpool. She was to have been preserved at Barrow-in-Furness. (© Sandy McClearn – smcclearn.smugmug.com)

The torpedo ready room looking aft aboard the submarine HMS *Onyx* showing rear doors of the six torpedo tubes. (© Sandy McClearn – smcclearn.smugmug.com)

risk to himself. In addition, some of the cylinder heads on one diesel engine had to be changed. The *Onyx* conducted the final stages of her long voyage mainly submerged to keep her presence a secret from the enemy.

Due to their comparatively enormous size, the Royal Navy's nuclear-powered submarines were unable to work close inshore and, as this conflict involved the landing of special forces on Argentine soil as well as on the islands themselves, the much smaller *Onyx* was pressed into this service, landing SAS and SBS troops that she had embarked at Ascension to carry out several covert missions. On one such occasion *Onyx* ran aground on an uncharted reef but managed to

extricate herself with only minor damage to her bows. A less attractive job was the despatching of the burnt-out hulk of Royal Fleet Auxiliary Landing Ship, Logistic *Sir Galahad*, which had been bombed and badly damaged by the resulting fires with heavy loss of life at Bluff Cove during the final stages of the war. At the end of July she sailed for home once more having sailed a total of 32,186.88km (20,000 miles) during the operation.

The *Onyx* was refitted at Rosyth following her return from the war and later that year returned to the South Atlantic again for five months during her fourth commission. Her task was reinforcing the South Atlantic Patrol in case the Argentine

Junta decided to chance their arm once more. On Trafalgar Day the captured Argentine Navy transport *Bahia Buen Suceso* was used as target practice for the surface fleet and then finally despatched by a torpedo from the *Onyx*, the sinking wreck being depth-charged on its way to the bottom. Following that *Onyx* served for a time with the Royal Canadian Navy, returning to Gosport again to pay off on 14 December 1990.

Due to one of the endless rounds of defence cuts that have followed each other with depressing succession since 1945, the *Onyx* was stricken from the Royal Navy along with her surviving sisters in 1991. Fortunately the Warship Preservation Trust stepped in and took her under their wing, making her part of their collection assembled at Birkenhead. She was placed on public display for several years, but, unfortunately, this organisation ultimately went into receivership and the various ships were left to their fates.

The *Onyx* was rescued for a second time by a businessman from Barrow-in-Furness, Mr Joe Mullen, who purchased her for £100,000 as a gift to his native town. On 30 June 2006 she was towed to the docks in Cumbria to become the main attraction at the newly-established Charitable Trust, The Submarine Heritage Centre museum complex, as a celebration of Barrow's long shipbuilding history, they having been building submarines for over a century. However, at the time of writing the website is closed down, e-mails go unanswered and rumours abound that she is to be towed to Ireland and scrapped. Sadly, by the time this book appears we may have lost her also.

In addition to the *Onyx* and *Ocelot*, Oberon-class submarines that have been preserved are the *Otus* at Sassnitz, Rügen, Germany, five boats, or surviving sections of boats, that later served with the Royal Australian Navy, *Onslow*, *Otway*, *Otama*, *Oxley* and *Orion* as well as the former Canadian vessels *Ojibwa* (originally to have been named *Onyx* for the RN but transferred while building), *Okanagan* and *Onodaga* and the ex-British *Olympus*.

MTB-102

The descendants of the Great War coastal motor boats (CMBs) were the motor torpedo boats and they served in their dozens with the Royal Navy Coastal Forces with distinction throughout the Second World War in the English Channel, the North Sea and in the Mediterranean. This boat was the first of her type, being built pre-war in 1937 as a speculation by Vosper Ltd, and being dubbed the Vosper Private Venture Boat. The Managing Director of Vosper, Commander Peter Du Cane CBE, felt sure there would be a need for such boats in large numbers and he was proved correct. She had a length of 21m (68ft) a beam of 4.50m (14ft 9in) and a 1.14m (3ft 9in) draft. Her wooden hull was a compound of double diagonal Honduras mahogany on Canadian rock elm. She

The *MTB-102*, first of her kind and veteran of Dunkirk, seen here at speed off Ramsgate in 2005 returning from Dunkirk Memorial service. (Copyright & Courtesy of Richard Basey, The MTB102 Trust)

was equipped with three 1,100hp Isotta-Fraschini 57-litre petrol engines, which gave her a nominal speed of 48 knots in light condition and 43 knots when fully equipped. Her armament initially comprised a solitary torpedo fired through a bow hatch with a re-load carried on rail aft, but trials showed better results could be achieved by launching both from a pair of 530mm (21-inch) torpedo tubes located either side of the vessel, vented at a 10-degree angle. She could also carry light machine guns for defence, and depth-charges. The boat was also used to trial a single 20mm Oerlikon gun.

She was purchased by the Admiralty and commissioned as *MTB-102*. She had a crew of two officers and eight men. Her early wartime service was in the Channel and under the command of Lieutenant Christopher Dreyer; she had the distinction of taking part in the Dunkirk evacuation in 1940, when she made a total of eight crossings. Admiral Wake-Walker, the Rear Admiral in charge afloat off the beaches, was forced to transfer to her when his flagship, the Flotilla Leader *Keith*, was sunk by Ju87 Stukas off the beaches, and conducted the last two nights' operations from her. In 1943 she was seconded to No. 615 Water Transport Company, RASC, who named her *Vimy*. In June 1944 she achieved fame by embarking Premier Winston Churchill and Allied Commander-in-Chief General Dwight Eisenhower when they inspected the assembled invasion fleet prior to the D-Day landings in Normandy. Post-war, she was sold out of service and became a private vessel.

The civilian owner equipped her with more economical Perkins P6 diesel engines for her voyages around the east coast but, with two decades in this role, she was sold again, becoming a houseboat on the Norfolk Broads and was largely forgotten. In 1973 a scout group found her in a semi-derelict state and finally some action was taken to save this unique little vessel, by then the only Royal Navy Dunkirk survivor. She was saved in 1976 when Kelso Films invested funds to refurbish her for a 'starring' role in the film they were making of the book *The Eagle Has Landed*, which starred Michael Caine. Another film, *Survival Run*, followed and, in her restored state, she attended HM Queen Elizabeth's Silver Jubilee Pageant on the Thames. In 2012 she was selected to attend the Diamond Jubilee Pageant on the Thames and lead the flotilla of Dunkirk Little Ships as the mount of the Commodore ADLS. She was refurbished again in 1983 and had a pair of new turbo-charged V8 engines presented by Perkins in 1985. She required yet further work in 1990 and, although she took part in the TV series 'Classic Ships', she required another set of engines in 2002, a pair of 600hp Cummins L10. She is kept in good seagoing order by the MTB-102 Trust, 3 Sea Lake Road, Oulton Broad, Lowestoft. Tel: 01502 57444.

FOXTROT-8

This little vessel is officially classed as a Landing Craft Assault (LCA) and was one of a quartet carried aboard the Assault Ship HMS *Fearless*. They could be considered to be descendants of the Second World War LCAs, or Higgins boats as the American termed them, which participated in all the major amphibious operations in the Mediterranean and Europe.

The *Foxtrot-8* and her sisters were constructed by the shipbuilders Camper & Nicholson at their Gosport works in 1959–60. They were constructed from marine ply on top of a hardwood frame. The troop-deck and the after conning tower were bulletproof-steel plated. Their dimensions were an overall length of 13.106m (43ft) and a waterline length of 11.582m (38ft), with a 3.048m (10ft 6in) beam. Their height was 2.743m (9ft) to the top of the forward ramp and the after conning tower and their weight was 12.5 tons. They had as their main power plant two Foden diesel engines (similar to those which powered the London Routemaster double-decker buses of the time) driving propellers which were safely housed inside tunnels at the stern of the craft. They were used to deploy Royal Marine Commandos onto shallow landing beaches and could carry up to thirty-five fully-equipped Royal Marines or a Land Rover and a towed trailer. They were carried on davits, two to port and two to starboard of each assault ship.

The *F-8* herself saw combat in the Falklands War in the South Atlantic between April and June 1982 when the *Fearless* was part of the Royal Navy Task Force that carried out Operation CORPORATE which freed the islands from Argentine invasion forces. They were deployed when 3 Commando Brigade and the Parachute Regiment were landed on *Blue* Beach at San Carlos on 21 May 1982. The *F-7* earned fame when, under the inspired leadership of Royal Marine Coxswain Corporal Alan White, she was instrumental in saving forty-one of the crew from the burning and sinking frigate *Antelope* when a UXB (unexploded bomb) aboard her detonated while it was being defused. The *F-7* herself had a very luck escape when an Argentine Navy A-4 Skyhawk fighter-bomber was shot down and crashed into the sea very close to her. The LCVPs proved invaluable with their shallow draft and,

Internal detail showing neglect of the landing craft assault (LCA) *Foxtrot-8*, in poor condition moored in the Mast Pond at Portsmouth Dockyard, October 2011 awaiting proper restoration (World Copyright 2012 Peter C. Smith)

as well as landing combat troops, they served as supply boats to reinforce the build-up, and even as makeshift mine clearance craft.

After the war *F-7* was put on permanent static display on the grass in front of the Royal Marines'

Museum, Eastney. *F-8* ended up with Hughes Marine Services, a salvage yard but was purchased by the Portsmouth Naval Base Property Trust (PNBPT) in 1997. She languished in the Mast Pond at Portsmouth Dockyard in a semi-derelict

Ramp to stern view of the landing craft assault (LCA) *Foxtrot-8*, in poor condition moored in the Mast Pond at Portsmouth Dockyard, October 2011 awaiting proper restoration (World Copyright 2012 Peter C. Smith)

state for some time, sunk by the stern and very forlorn. More recently she was refloated and awaits a proper overhaul when Boathouse No. 4 becomes free. There is said to be a third LCVP in a similar state, *Tango-5*, which served aboard the *Intrepid*, the sister ship of the *Fearless*, but I have not seen her.

Among the very many other interesting vessels that the PNBPT administers are the motor gunboat *MGB-81*, the RAF high speed launch (HSL) *102*, which were used from 1937 and performed air-sea rescue missions during the Second World War, and the Fast Motor Boat *43957*.

OTHER PRESERVED VESSELS

This list is by no means intended to be exhaustive because vessels are in a constant state of flux with new acquisitions arriving on the scene, while, sadly, lack of funding, sales or scrapping means a steady flow of historic maritime history disappears for good. This latter trend has accelerated in the last two years due to Government constraints on funding. Some consider this short-sighted in the long term, but, once a vessel has gone, she is gone for good no matter what the reason.

Amy Howson – an iron-hulled keel, originally built at the Joss Scarr's shipyard at Beverley in 1914, with the iron hull for George Robert 'Cuckoo' Scaife, being named *Sophia*, in honour of his wife. She traded as a collier in Yorkshire until 1916. On being sold to Gouldthorpe, Wright and Scott she was re-rigged to become a Humber sloop and worked continually with varied cargoes until 1924 on the Humber and between Grimsby and Hull. Purchased by W. H. Barraclough and re-named *Amy Howson*, she was used to convey a wide variety of cargoes in northern England until she finally ceased trading in 1973. The Humber Keel & Sloop Preservation Society restored her between 1975 and 1981 and she is currently moored at King's Straithe.

Auld Reekie – represents the scores of immortal 'Clyde Puffers' which carried coal and other cargo down the Clyde and around the Western Isles from the late 1800s onward, and later took the crews of the warships of both the Grand Fleet in the First World War and the Home Fleet in the Second from harbour to the ships. They were given a place in history with the publication of Neil Munro's *Vital Spark* stories. The name 'Puffer' itself comes from the characteristic black smoke emissions from the funnels when the coal-fired steam from the engine was vented in staccato

bursts like a railway locomotive. *Auld Reekie* herself, however, was *not* Scottish built but constructed south of the border at Northwich, by J. Pimblott shipbuilders on the Weaver River as late as 1942. She was originally given the number VIC-27 which reflected her role (Victualing Inshore Craft) and that of her fifty-nine similar vessels, as victualing boats fitted with freshwater tanks. But her design was solidly based on that of those puffers built by J. & J. Hay of Glasgow. She has a length of 20.36m (66.8ft), a beam of 5.638m (18.5ft) and a 2.438m (8ft) draught, is of 96-GRT and powered by a compound two-cylinder engine.

The Admiralty kept her gainfully employed for forty years, ending her Navy service at Rosyth until she was laid up in 1962 at Ardrossan. Here she was found by Sir James Miller who bought her from Glenburn Shipping. He had her converted as a charter ship and was to have named her *Maggie*, but finally she received the impromptu but suitable name *Auld Reekie* in 1969. After a period at Oban as a tender for the Land, Sea and Air Youth Club and starring in the title role of Munro's books as a television series, she underwent extensive restoration at the Crinan Shipyard.

Barnabas – a St Ives, Cornwall, fishing lugger, known as a double-ended mackerel driver built by Henry Trevorrow at Porthgwidded, St Ives, for Barnabas Thomas and first registered in October 1881. Once there were a thousand such vessels, lug-rigged seine- and drift-net mackerel and herring fishing boats, based on Cornish ports but now *Barnabas* is one of the very few still existing. She has a length overall of 12.192m (40ft), a beam of 3.535m (11ft 6in) and a 1.828m (6ft) draught, with a displacement of 11.7 tons. She was termed a 'Dipping Lugger' from her particular rig but in 1917 she had the luxury of a 26hp engine added as auxiliary power. She had a crew of five men and a boy and fished a wide area, from the Isles of Scilly to near Dublin Bay.

She fished until 1954 before being sold and used as a yacht for a period. In 1970 she was taken over by the National Maritime Trust by Mr Peter Cadbury, one of her former owners, and was refitted at a shipyard on the River Dart by Westward TV and returned to her original state. In 1994 the Cornish Maritime Trust bought her for the nominal sum of £1 and in 1996 a new engine was fitted. More work was required, however, and, in 2005, the Heritage Lottery Fund awarded her a sufficient sum to bring her back to full seagoing potential. By 2008 the work was completed and she now works from both Penzance and Newlyn Bay during the summer months.

Centaur – a Thames spritsail ketch-rig wooden sailing barge of 65 tons built at Harwich in 1895 and worked under sail for the following sixty years, commercially until 1950 and then as a Maldon-based charter vessel until bought by the Thames Sailing Barge Trust in 1974. Extensively restored between 1977 and 1993 she is now employed as a weekend sailing and charter vessel along the south-eastern coast.

Coastal Motor Boat No. 4 – the Great War forerunners of the famous motor torpedo boats (MTBs) and motor gunboats (MGBs) of the Second World War and the fast patrol boats of the 1950s–60s. They were designed by John I. Thorneycroft's shipyard. This particular craft is that in which Lieutenant Augustus Agar gained the Victoria Cross for sinking the Bolshevik cruiser *Oleg* in 1919. Restored and on display at the Imperial War Museum, Duxford, Cambridge.

Comrade – Humber steel-hulled keel, built by Warren at New Holland, Hull, for Turner Carmichael in 1923 and originally named *Wanda*. She traded barley and coal before being sold to John Taylor who renamed her for his wife as *Ada Carter*. Sold again in 1929 to Arthur Schofield, Beverley and renamed *Comrade*, she was used for mixed cargo trading. Purchased in 1974 by The Humber Keel & Sloop Preservation Society and subsequently restored by them, she has successfully sailed many thousands of miles since.

Earl of Pembroke – this magnificent tall ship, a 350-ton, three-masted barque, was built by Albert Svenson at Pukavik, Sweden in 1948 under the name *Orion*. Of some 174 GRT, she has an overall length of 44.2m (143ft), a beam of 7.3m (24ft), a draught of 3.20m (10.5ft), a mast height of 28m (91ft 10in) and a sail area of 883m^2. She also has a MAN 6-cylinder 300hp engine driving a three-bladed propeller and has a crew of fifteen. She was used in the timber trade between the Baltic and the east coast for many years but in 1974 was laid up in Denmark. Five years' idleness followed and then she was bought by Square Sail, her present owners, in 1979 and underwent a six-year total restoration to return her to her former glory.

She is now based at St Austell, Cornwall and is utilised for sail training and for charter voyages around the UK and to Europe. Her accommodation comprises four 2-berth and one 4-berth cabins. In addition she has 'starred' in the following motion pictures down the years – *Treasure Island*, *A Respectable Trade*, *Moll Flanders*, *Cutthroat Island*, *Frenchman's Creek*, *Shaka Zulu*, *Longitude*, *Wives and Daughters* and *Amazing Grace*.

Elswick No. 2 – the Tyne wherries were used for bringing Tyneside coal downriver to the colliers, originally under tow of tugs as dumb lighters, and replaced the smaller Tyne keels in that work. They now have only one survivor and, although not very attractive, it is important for that reason. She is a shell-clinker-built, 55-ton (49,895.161kg) vessel with a length of 17.37m (55ft) and a beam of 7.01m (23ft). Her later owners, Vickers Scotswood, fitted her with a small motor and used her as a 'putter' to transport heavy machinery. Post the Second World War, she was bought by N. Keedy and Sons and used to transport steel sections when there was still shipbuilding on the Tyne. By 1970 she was the sole survivor of many hundreds of such vessels and was donated to the Maritime Trust.

Other Preserved Vessels

She is owned by the Tyne & Wear Museum who took her over in 1976, and kept her at Hebburn/Jarrow and then to the Beamish Museum where she is in the Large Objects Store and, unfortunately, *not* on display to visitors.

Kelvinhugh Ferry No. 8 – built by H. McLean, Renfrew in 1951 as the *Ferry Queen* for the Clydeport, Glasgow and a typical Clyde diesel-engined ferry with the capacity for 144 passengers. Finally withdrawn from service in 1980, she was saved by the Forth & Clyde Canal Society and ran excursions between Kirkintilloch and Maryhill before returning to the Clyde. In 1999 she was taken over by the Clyde Maritime Trust and restored. Currently berthed near to The Tall Ship *Glenlee* and still actively employed.

Kindly Light – built in 1911 at a cost of £500 by Armour Brothers at Fleetwood, to the design of William Stoba, this sailing pilot cutter was one of 200 in service in the Bristol Channel at the turn of the twentieth century. She had a deck length of 16.154m (53ft 6in), a beam of 4.267m (14ft 6in), a draft of 2.438m (8ft 6in) and a displacement of 33 tons.

She is currently located at Gweek, Helston, Cornwall, under the ownership of Malcolm J. McKeand of the Bristol Channel Pilot Cutter Owners' Association. She has spent eighteen years undergoing restoration to her totally original form at the hands of Master Boat Builder David Walkey at Porthleven in time for her centenary in November 2011.

Provident – this famous Brixham sailing gaff-rigged ketch was originally built by J. Sanders, Galmpton, in 1924, being one of the very last 'Mule' type sailing trawlers ever constructed. She is of 78 tons, with an overall length of 27.56m (90ft 5in) and a waterline length of 18.29m (60ft). After only a few years service she was sold and converted into a private yacht, in which condition she remained until 1952. A Salcombe organisation, The Island Cruising Club, then took her over. She has subsequently been widely used as a charter and sail-training boat with accommoda-tion for up to twelve guests and four crew and all modern navigation aids.

Robin – what is described as the world's oldest complete steam-coaster, the SS *Robin*, is, at 120 years of age, one of the oldest steam-driven vessels still in an entire state. The last representative of thousands upon thousands of coasters, the forgotten little ships that plied their trade up and down the littoral of the UK and Europe for many decades and kept the cogs of industry turning, ignored and belittled, but essential. John Masefield gave them their epitaph in his poem *Cargoes* many years ago and his immortal words reflect their humdrum service:

Dirty British coaster with a salt-caked smoke stack,
Butting through the Channel in the mad March days,
With a cargo of Tyne coal,
Road-rails, pig-lead,
Firewood, iron-ware, and cheap tin trays.

Now just the *Robin* survives to give people an insight into how they worked. She was built by the Thames Ironworks and Shipbuilding and Engineering Company Ltd, at Orchard House Yard, in Bow Creek off the Thames in 1890, one of a pair of identical ships (the other was *Rook*) destined for Mackenzie Macaloine and Robert Thomson for Ponsonby and Company of Newport. She was of 366 GRT, with a 44m (144ft) overall length, has a beam of 7m (23ft) and a 3.7m (12.2ft) draught. She was powered with a 60hp 3-cylinder triple-expansion reciprocating engine, built by Gourlay Brothers at Dundee where it was installed, and which gave her a speed of 10 knots; this engine still survives. She had a crew of twelve and made her first voyage on 20 December 1890.

She was sold two years later to Andrew Forrester Blackwater and traded with very mixed cargoes from Glasgow, where she was still registered. Sold again in 1900 and renamed *Maria*, she served a succession of Spanish operators faithfully off the Spanish coast for seventy-five years. She was capable of hauling 400 tons of mixed cargo and underwent a late modernisation in 1966 which kept her working until 1972. Bought by the Maritime Trust in 1974 while awaiting her final voyage to the breakers' yard, she was restored prior to being moored at St Katherine's Dock near the Tower of London. Between 1991 and 2008 she was at West India Quay in the heart of the rejuvenated Docklands. In 2002 she was bought once more and the SS *Robin* Trust established and she became part of the Core Collection of the National Historic Fleet. The SS *Robin* project under David Kampfner was established and, despite being inexplicably refused National Lottery funding, *Robin* was again saved for posterity by a deal with Crossrail Legacy which saw £1.9 million loan funding made available to restore her at Lowestoft and provide a Polish-built floating dock in time for the London Olympics. She was moored at Tilbury for a period from 2010 but now has a permanent base at the Royal Docks. It is hoped that in 2012 she can be used as a photographic gallery and educational centre as well as a floating museum and archive.

Turbinia – this small experimental vessel was built in 1894 by Brown and Hood, Wallsend, and used solely to display the qualities of the first Parsons steam turbine which so revolutionised Royal Navy steam propulsion. She had a displacement of 44.5 tons, a length of 31.93m (104ft 9in), a beam of 2.7m (9ft) and a 0.9144m (3ft) draught. Although initially her three-stage axial-flow direct acting steam turbines, which drove three shafts, were not successful, due to cavitation of her propeller, later she achieved the phenomenal speed of 34.5 knots.

She caught the public attention when she could not be caught at the June 1897 Spithead Naval Review as she blatantly, and illegally, steamed up and down between the lines of warships. This forced the Admiralty to build two experimental destroyers *Cobra* and *Viper* in 1899 to test for themselves Parsons' invention. She was later exhibited at the Paris Exhibition in 1900, a disloyal act of commercialism in itself, but by that time Germany was beginning to replace France as the traditional enemy sea power. By 1905 the Admiralty had totally embraced the concept and other navies duly followed.

By 1926 she was in poor condition and was kept ashore before being offered as a gift to the Science Museum in South Kensington. She had to be bisected as she proved too large to exhibit as a whole. The front section was sent north to Newcastle in 1944, later followed in 1959 by the after section and a re-built centre section which was displayed at the Newcastle Municipal Museum of Science and Industry. In 1983 she was reconstructed entirely and in 1996 she was moved to The Military Vehicle Museum and then, more recently, transferred yet again to the local Science Museum where she currently resides.